VERONA

POCKET TRAVEL GUIDE 2024

Explore History, Culture, Hidden Gems, Cuisine and Local Secrets in the Largest City Municipality in the Region of Northeastern Italy – Packed with Detailed Maps & Travel Itineraries

BY

MICHAEL VIANNEY

Copyright © 2024 Michael Vianney. All rights reserved. The entirety of this material, encompassing text, visuals, and other multimedia elements, is the intellectual property of Michael Vianney and is safeguarded by copyright legislation and global agreements. No segment of this content may be replicated, shared, or transmitted in any form or via any medium without explicit written authorization from Michael Vianney. Unauthorized utilization, replication, or dispersal of this content may result in legal repercussions, encompassing civil and criminal penalties. For queries regarding permissions or additional information, kindly contact the author via the provided contact details in the publication or on the author's official page.

TABLE OF CONTENTS

Copyright..1

My Experience in Verona...5

Benefits of this Guide...7

Chapter 1. Introduction to Verona..10

1.1 History and Culture...10

1.2 Geography, Climate and Best Time to Visit....................................11

1.3 Overview of Verona Neighborhood...13

1.3 Local Customs and Etiquette..15

Chapter 2. Accommodation Options..17

2.1 Hotels in Verona City Center..18

2.2 Bed and Breakfasts and Guesthouses...20

2.3 Boutique Hotels and Luxury Resorts..23

2.4 Apartment Rentals and Vacation Homes...25

2.5 Unique Accommodations: Agriturismo and Vineyard Stays...........28

Chapter 3. Transportation in Verona...31

3.1 Getting to Verona..31

3.2 Public Transport: Bus and Metro..32

3.3 Taxis and Ride-Sharing Services...33

3.4 Renting a Car or Scooter...36

3.5 Exploring on Foot: Walking Tours and Bike Rentals......................39

Chapter 4. Top 10 Hidden Gem Attractions..42

4.1 Giardino Giusti..43

4.2 Castelvecchio Museum..46

4.3 Ponte Pietra...49

4.4 Scaliger Tombs..52

4.5 Basilica di San Zeno Maggiore...55

4.6 Piazza delle Erbe Market...58

4.7 Roman Theater and Archaeological Museum..............................61

4.8 Juliet's Tomb...64

4.9 Teatro Romano...65

4.10 Borgo Trento District..68

4.11 Sports, Outdoor Activities and Adventures.............................70

4.12 Recommended Tour Operators and Guided Tours...................72

Chapter 5 Practical Information and Travel Resources.....................75

5.1 Maps and Navigation..76

5.2 Five Days Itinerary...78

5.3 Essential Packing List..79

5.4 Visa Requirements and Entry Procedures..................................81

5.5 Safety Tips and Emergency Contacts...82

5.6 Currency Exchange and Banking Services.................................84

5.7 Language, Communication and Useful Phrases.........................87

5.8 Shopping and Souvenirs...89

5.9 Health and Wellness Centers..93

5.10 Useful Websites, Mobile Apps and Online Resources............95

5.11 Internet Access and Connectivity...96

5.12 Visitor Centers and Tourist Assistance....................................98

Chapter 6. Culinary Delights...101

6.1 Traditional Veronese Cuisine: Risotto and Pastissada de Caval................. 101

6.2 Trattorias and Osterias..104

6.3 Wine Tasting Tours in Valpolicella...106

6.4 Gelaterias and Dessert Shops..109

6.5 Coffee Culture: Caffè Espresso and Aperitivo Hour................111

6.6 Best Fine Dining Restaurants..114

Chapter 7. Day Trips and Excursions..118

7.1 Lake Garda: Sirmione and Garda Town....................................119

7.2 Vicenza and Palladian Villas...121

7.3 Mantua: Ducal Palace and Palazzo Te.....................................122

7.4 Venice: The Floating City..124

7.5 Soave and Wine Country...126

Chapter 8. Entertainment and Nightlife..128

8.1 Piazza Bra: Bars and Terraces..128

8.2 Opera at the Arena di Verona...131

8.3 Live Music Venues and Jazz Clubs...132

8.4 Nightlife in Veronetta and Piazza delle Erbe.............................134

8.5 Cultural Events: Festivals and Concerts....................................136

Conclusion and Recommendations...138

MY EXPERIENCE IN VERONA

There's a magical quality to Verona that's hard to put into words. It's more than just a city in Italy, it's a living, breathing storybook, where every street and ancient building whispers tales of romance, tragedy, and triumph. As a veteran traveler and author who believes in experiencing a place firsthand before writing about it, my time in Verona was nothing short of enchanting. The warm Italian sun casting a golden glow over the terracotta rooftops, the sound of laughter and music echoing through narrow alleys, and the scent of freshly baked bread and rich espresso lingering in the air. That's the Verona I fell in love with, and I'm convinced that anyone who visits will feel the same. From the iconic Verona Arena, a breathtaking Roman amphitheater that still hosts concerts and events today, to the majestic Castelvecchio, a medieval castle with a storied past, the city is a treasure trove of historical wonders. I took a stroll through the bustling Piazza delle Erbe, where market stalls sell everything from fresh produce to handmade crafts, or wander along the tranquil banks of the Adige River, where locals gather to relax and soak in the beauty of their surroundings.

Of course, no visit to Verona would be complete without experiencing its most famous literary legacy: Shakespeare's Romeo and Juliet. As I stood on the balcony of Juliet's house, surrounded by lovelorn tourists snapping photos and leaving heartfelt notes, I couldn't help but be swept up in the timeless romance of it all. Whether or not you believe in the legend of the star-crossed lovers, there's something undeniably magical about being in the presence of such enduring literary history. But Verona isn't just a city of romance, it's also a culinary paradise. From mouthwatering pasta dishes to decadent gelato, every meal is a feast for the senses. One of my favorite memories from my time in Verona is sipping on a glass of local wine at a charming osteria, surrounded by friendly locals and delicious food. There's something truly special about the way food brings people together in this city, and I can't wait to return and indulge in more culinary delights.

One of my most memorable experiences in Verona was stumbling upon a hidden courtyard tucked away behind a nondescript doorway. As I sat surrounded by blooming flowers and ancient stone walls, I felt like I had uncovered a secret world just waiting to be explored. But perhaps the most unforgettable aspect of my time in Verona was the people. From the warm-hearted locals who welcomed me with open arms to the fellow travelers I met along the way, the sense of community and camaraderie in this city is truly unparalleled. Whether I was sharing stories over a meal or dancing the night away in a lively piazza, I felt a connection to Verona and its people that will stay with me forever.

BENEFITS OF THIS GUIDE

Verona stands as a testament to the rich tapestry of culture, history, and romance that defines this enchanting region. Immortalized by Shakespeare's timeless tragedy, "Romeo and Juliet," Verona beckons travelers from across the globe with its captivating blend of ancient ruins, Renaissance architecture, and vibrant streets pulsating with life.

Maps and Navigation

Navigating the charming streets of Verona is a delightful experience, with its compact size making it easily walkable. Visitors can explore the city's historic center, a UNESCO World Heritage Site, where every cobblestone alley and Renaissance square reveals a new facet of its rich heritage. For those who prefer guided tours, numerous companies offer walking tours led by knowledgeable locals, providing insights into the city's history and culture.

Accommodation Options

Verona caters to a wide range of travelers, offering accommodations to suit every budget and preference. From luxurious boutique hotels nestled in historic palazzos to cozy bed and breakfasts tucked away in quiet corners, the city boasts a plethora of options for lodging. For those seeking a truly immersive experience, staying in one of the many charming guesthouses within the historic center allows guests to soak in the atmosphere of this ancient city.

Transportation

Verona benefits from excellent transportation connections, with its international airport serving as a gateway for travelers arriving from all corners of the globe. For those arriving by train, Verona Porta Nuova station provides easy access to the city center and surrounding areas. Within the city, an efficient public transportation network of buses and taxis ensures convenient travel for visitors.

Top Attractions

Verona is a treasure trove of attractions, each more captivating than the last. The iconic Arena di Verona, a Roman amphitheater dating back to the 1st century, is a must-visit, hosting world-class opera performances against the backdrop of ancient ruins. For a glimpse into the city's medieval past, a visit to the imposing Castelvecchio fortress is essential, while the romantic Juliet's House offers a chance to step into the world of Shakespearean tragedy.

Practical Information and Travel Resources

Before embarking on a journey to Verona, it is essential to familiarize oneself with practical information such as local customs, currency exchange, and emergency contact numbers. Travelers can also benefit from a wealth of online resources, including travel blogs, forums, and official tourism websites, offering insider tips and recommendations for making the most of their stay in Verona.

Culinary Delights

Verona's culinary scene is a feast for the senses, with its rich gastronomic heritage reflecting the diverse influences of Italian cuisine. From hearty pasta dishes served in traditional trattorias to delicate risottos infused with local flavors, Verona offers a culinary journey like no other. Visitors can also indulge in the region's world-renowned wines, with vineyards scattered throughout the surrounding countryside.

Culture and Heritage

Verona's cultural heritage is as diverse as it is rich, with a history spanning millennia and a legacy that has left its mark on every corner of the city. From the ancient Roman ruins of the Forum to the grandeur of Renaissance palaces, Verona's architectural wonders tell the story of its illustrious past. Art lovers will also find much to admire in the city's museums and galleries, which house masterpieces by renowned artists such as Titian and Veronese.

Outdoor Activities and Adventures

For those seeking adventure amidst Verona's stunning natural landscapes, the nearby Lake Garda offers a plethora of outdoor activities, from hiking and cycling to sailing and windsurfing. The surrounding countryside is also dotted with picturesque vineyards and olive groves, perfect for leisurely strolls and wine tasting tours.

Shopping

Verona is a shopper's paradise, with its charming streets lined with an array of boutiques, artisanal shops, and bustling markets. From designer fashion and leather goods to handmade crafts and souvenirs, Verona offers something for every taste and budget. Visitors can also explore the city's vibrant food markets, where they can sample local delicacies and fresh produce.

Day Trips and Excursions

Verona's strategic location makes it an ideal base for exploring the surrounding region, with numerous day trip options available for travelers. From the picturesque towns of Lake Garda to the historic cities of Venice and Milan, Verona offers endless opportunities for exploration and discovery.

Entertainment and Nightlife

As the sun sets over the city, Verona comes alive with an array of entertainment options to suit every taste. From cozy wine bars and traditional osterias to lively nightclubs and music venues, Verona's nightlife scene offers something for everyone. Visitors can also catch a performance at one of the city's theaters or enjoy an evening stroll along the picturesque riverfront.

CHAPTER 1
INTRODUCTION TO VERONA

1.1 History and Culture

Verona's origins can be traced back to ancient times, with evidence of human settlement dating as far back as the 6th century BC. Its strategic location along the Adige River made it a coveted prize for various civilizations, including the Romans, who established it as a flourishing colony in the 1st century BC. Under Roman rule, Verona thrived as a bustling trade hub and a center of culture and commerce in the region. The legacy of Roman rule is still palpable in Verona today, with iconic landmarks such as the Arena di Verona standing as a testament to the city's ancient heritage. This remarkably preserved Roman amphitheater, located in the heart of Verona's historic center, serves as a reminder of the city's illustrious past and continues to host world-class performances.

Beyond its Roman roots, Verona's cultural tapestry is also woven with threads of medieval splendor. The city's historic center, a UNESCO World Heritage Site, is a labyrinth of narrow streets and charming piazzas lined with centuries-old buildings, each bearing witness to the rich history that has shaped Verona into the captivating city it is today. One cannot explore Verona without encountering the legendary tale of Romeo and Juliet, immortalized by William Shakespeare. While the story itself is fictional, Verona's connection to the tragic lovers is very real. Casa di Giulietta, or Juliet's House, is a pilgrimage site for romantics from around the world, who come to pay homage to the iconic balcony where Romeo is said to have declared his love for Juliet. The house, with its iconic balcony and courtyard adorned with love letters, serves as a poignant reminder of the enduring power of love and tragedy.

Verona's cultural heritage extends beyond its architectural marvels to its vibrant culinary scene, which reflects the diverse influences that have shaped the city's identity over the centuries. From traditional trattorias serving hearty Venetian fare to chic cafes and wine bars offering a taste of modern Italian cuisine, Verona is a gastronomic paradise waiting to be explored. But perhaps what truly sets Verona apart is its timeless charm and the warmth of its people. As you wander through its winding streets and bustling squares, you'll be greeted with smiles and hospitality at every turn, inviting you to immerse yourself in the magic of this enchanting city.

1.2 Geography, Climate and Best Time to Visit

Situated along the Adige River, Verona boasts a strategic location that has made it a crossroads of trade and culture for centuries. The city's geography is characterized by rolling hills, fertile plains, and a stunning backdrop of the Italian Alps in the distance.

Climate

Verona experiences a temperate climate, with distinct seasons offering visitors a variety of experiences throughout the year. Understanding the weather patterns of each season is essential for planning the perfect visit to this enchanting city.

Spring (March-May): Spring is a delightful time to visit Verona, as the city comes alive with blooming flowers and warmer temperatures. Average highs range from 15°C to 20°C (59°F to 68°F), making it ideal for outdoor exploration. However, it's worth noting that spring showers are common, so packing an umbrella is advisable.

Summer (June-August): Summer in Verona is characterized by long, sunny days and balmy evenings. Average temperatures soar to around 28°C to 30°C (82°F to 86°F), making it perfect for soaking up the sun in one of the city's many charming piazzas or enjoying a leisurely stroll along the riverbanks. However, it can get quite hot, so staying hydrated and seeking shade when necessary is essential.

Autumn (September-November): Autumn brings cooler temperatures and fewer crowds to Verona, making it an ideal time for those who prefer a more relaxed atmosphere. Average highs range from 17°C to 22°C (63°F to 72°F), and the changing foliage adds a touch of vibrant color to the cityscape. While rain is more frequent in the autumn months, the crisp air and beautiful scenery make it a wonderful time to visit.

Winter (December-February): Winter in Verona is mild compared to many other European cities, with average temperatures hovering around 5°C to 10°C (41°F to 50°F). While snow is rare, visitors can expect some chilly days and occasional rain showers. However, the festive atmosphere of the holiday season and lower tourist numbers make winter an appealing time to experience Verona's charm.

Best Times to Visit Verona

Determining the best time to visit Verona depends largely on personal preferences and interests. For those who enjoy mild weather and blooming flowers, spring is an excellent choice. Summer is perfect for sun-seekers and those who want to experience the city's vibrant outdoor culture. Autumn offers a quieter, more contemplative atmosphere, while winter provides a magical backdrop for holiday festivities. In addition to considering the weather, visitors should also take into account major events and festivals happening in Verona throughout the year. The renowned Verona Opera Festival, held in the ancient Roman amphitheater during the summer months, is a highlight for music lovers from around the world. Other popular events include the Vinitaly wine fair in April and the Christmas markets in December.

1.3 Overview of Verona Neighborhood

Verona is a city of diverse neighborhoods, each offering its own unique charm and character. From historic squares to lively markets, there's something to discover around every corner. Let's take a closer look at Verona's most enchanting neighborhoods, each with its own story to tell.

Centro Storico (Historic Center): Located at the heart of Verona, Centro Storico is a labyrinth of narrow streets and hidden squares that transport visitors back in time. Here, you'll find iconic landmarks such as the Verona Arena, a magnificent Roman amphitheater that hosts concerts and events throughout the year. Wander through Piazza delle Erbe, a bustling market square filled with colorful stalls selling everything from fresh produce to artisanal crafts. Don't miss the chance to explore Juliet's House, where the legendary lovers Romeo and Juliet supposedly lived, and leave a message on the famous balcony for good luck in love.

San Zeno: Tucked away on the outskirts of the city, San Zeno is a peaceful neighborhood known for its stunning basilica and tranquil atmosphere. The highlight of this area is the Basilica di San Zeno Maggiore, a Romanesque church dating back to the 10th century. Step inside to admire the breathtaking frescoes and sculptures, or simply relax in the adjacent square and soak in the beauty of the surrounding architecture. San Zeno offers a welcome respite from the hustle and bustle of the city center, making it the perfect place to unwind and reflect.

Veronetta: Situated on the left bank of the Adige River, Veronetta is a vibrant neighborhood beloved by locals and visitors alike. Here, you'll find charming cafes, trendy boutiques, and a lively student population that infuses the area with energy and vitality. Take a leisurely stroll along the riverbanks and watch as locals gather to socialize and enjoy the sunshine. Don't miss the chance to visit the Giardino Giusti, a stunning Renaissance garden that offers panoramic views of the city below. Veronetta is the perfect place to experience Verona like a true local, immersing yourself in the city's rich culture and vibrant street life.

Borgo Trento: Located just north of the historic center, Borgo Trento is a bustling residential neighborhood with a distinctly modern flair. Here, you'll find wide boulevards lined with elegant shops and restaurants, as well as leafy parks where locals gather to relax and unwind. The highlight of this area is the Ospedale Maggiore, a historic hospital turned cultural center that hosts art exhibitions, concerts, and other events throughout the year. Take some time to explore the charming side streets and hidden courtyards, where you'll discover a wealth of hidden gems waiting to be uncovered.

Borgo Venezia: Stretching to the east of the historic center, Borgo Venezia is a vibrant neighborhood known for its eclectic mix of cultures and cuisines. Here, you'll find bustling markets selling everything from fresh seafood to exotic spices, as well as a diverse array of restaurants and cafes serving up delicious international fare. Don't miss the chance to visit the Porta Vescovo, an ancient gate that once served as the entrance to the city. Borgo Venezia offers a taste of Verona's cosmopolitan spirit, making it a must-visit destination for food lovers and culture enthusiasts alike.

1.4 Local Customs and Etiquette

In Verona, every encounter begins with a heartfelt greeting, embodying the warmth and hospitality that define the city's spirit. Whether meeting a friend or making a new acquaintance, locals and visitors alike exchange warm embraces, handshakes, or kisses on the cheek, forging instant connections and fostering a sense of community. This cherished custom reflects the genuine warmth and friendliness of Veronese culture, inviting travelers to immerse themselves in the city's welcoming embrace from the moment they arrive.

Culinary Celebration

Dining in Verona is not merely a meal; it's a sensory journey infused with tradition, flavor, and conviviality. As visitors indulge in the city's culinary delights, they are invited to embrace the art of slow dining, savoring each delectable bite and engaging in lively conversation with fellow diners. From traditional trattorias serving hearty pasta dishes to quaint osterias offering locally sourced wines and cheeses, Verona's gastronomic scene is a celebration of life, community, and the rich tapestry of Italian cuisine.

Respect for Tradition

Verona's rich history and cultural heritage are woven into the very fabric of daily life, shaping the customs and traditions observed by its residents. From religious processions in historic churches to festive celebrations in ancient piazzas, the city's calendar is punctuated by rituals that honor its storied past. Visitors are invited to join in these time-honored traditions, experiencing firsthand the reverence and respect with which Veronese culture preserves its heritage for future generations to cherish.

Modesty in Religious Spaces

As visitors explore Verona's majestic churches and cathedrals, they are reminded of the city's deep-rooted spirituality and reverence for the divine. In these sacred spaces, it is customary to dress modestly and observe a respectful demeanor, paying homage to the religious traditions that have shaped Veronese culture for centuries. Whether attending a mass or admiring the exquisite artwork adorning the walls, visitors are invited to experience the tranquility and serenity of Verona's spiritual sanctuaries with humility and grace.

Art of Conversation

In Verona, conversation is more than just a means of communication; it's an art form that fosters connection, understanding, and camaraderie among friends and strangers alike. Whether sharing stories over a leisurely meal or engaging in spirited debates in a bustling piazza, the people of Verona embrace dialogue as a cornerstone of their culture, inviting visitors to join in the exchange of ideas and perspectives. Through the art of conversation, travelers can deepen their appreciation for Verona's rich tapestry of culture, history, and tradition, forging meaningful connections that endure long after their journey has ended.

CHAPTER 2
ACCOMMODATION OPTIONS

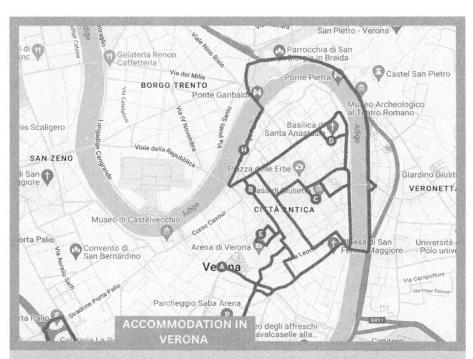

Directions from Verona, VR, Italy to Palazzo Victoria, Via Adua, Verona, VR, Italy

A	D	G
Verona, VR, Italy	Hotel Due Torri, Piazza Sant'anastasia, Verona, VR, Italy	La Corte di Giulietta Exclusive Suites, Inside Juliet's Courtyard, Via Cappello, Verona, VR, Italy

B	E	H
Palazzo Victoria, Via Adua, Verona, VR, Italy	Hotel Milano & SPA, Via Tre Marchetti, Verona, VR, Italy	B&B Casa Panvinio, Lungadige

C	F	I
Relais Balcone di Giulietta, Via Cappello, Verona, VR, Italy	Hotel Veronesi La Torre, Via Monte Baldo, Dossobuono, VR, Italy	Palazzo Victoria, Via Adua, Verona, VR, Italy

2.1 Hotels in Verona City Center

Each hotel in Verona boasts its own charm, offering a blend of luxurious accommodations, impeccable service, and unique amenities tailored to cater to the diverse needs of travelers. From historic palaces to contemporary boutique hotels, Verona's city center offers a range of options to suit every taste and preference.

Palazzo Victoria

Palazzo Victoria, situated in the vibrant Piazza delle Erbe, stands as a testament to Verona's rich heritage. This five-star hotel seamlessly blends Renaissance architecture with modern elegance, providing guests with a truly immersive experience. Accommodations at Palazzo Victoria range from deluxe rooms to opulent suites, each exquisitely furnished and equipped with state-of-the-art amenities. Guests can indulge in the hotel's Michelin-starred restaurant, featuring delectable Italian cuisine crafted from locally sourced ingredients. Additionally, Palazzo Victoria offers a wellness center, complete with a spa and fitness facilities, ensuring a rejuvenating stay for all visitors. For reservations and further information, visit the official website at www.palazzovictoria.com.

Relais de Charme Il Sogno di Giulietta

For those seeking a tranquil retreat amidst the bustling city center, Relais de Charme Il Sogno di Giulietta offers an enchanting escape. Located just steps away from Juliet's famous balcony, this boutique hotel captures the essence of romance and sophistication. Each room is elegantly appointed with antique furnishings and modern conveniences, providing guests with a luxurious haven to unwind after a day of exploration. The hotel's charming courtyard serves as the perfect spot to enjoy a leisurely breakfast or evening aperitif, surrounded by the timeless beauty of Verona. With personalized concierge services and exclusive access to Verona's most coveted attractions, Relais de Charme Il

Sogno di Giulietta ensures a truly unforgettable stay. For bookings and additional details, visit www.ilsognodigiulietta.com.

Hotel Due Torri

Steeped in history and elegance, Hotel Due Torri stands as a beacon of luxury in Verona's historic center. Housed within a meticulously restored 14th-century palazzo, this five-star hotel exudes old-world charm and sophistication at every turn. Guests can choose from a variety of sumptuously decorated rooms and suites, each offering panoramic views of the city skyline or the hotel's lush gardens. Hotel Due Torri boasts a range of exceptional amenities, including a rooftop terrace, gourmet restaurants, and a well-appointed spa, providing guests with the ultimate indulgence during their stay. With its unparalleled service and attention to detail, Hotel Due Torri ensures a truly memorable experience for discerning travelers. For reservations and more information, visit www.hotelduetorriverona.com.

Hotel Milano & Spa

Embrace the allure of contemporary luxury at Hotel Milano & Spa, conveniently located in the heart of Verona's historic center. This stylish boutique hotel offers sleek and modern accommodations, seamlessly blending comfort with sophistication. Each room is thoughtfully designed with chic furnishings and state-of-the-art amenities, ensuring a comfortable stay for every guest. Hotel Milano & Spa boasts an array of onsite facilities, including a rooftop terrace with panoramic views of the city, a fully equipped fitness center, and a tranquil spa offering a range of rejuvenating treatments. Guests can also indulge in gourmet cuisine at the hotel's restaurant, featuring innovative dishes inspired by traditional Italian flavors. With its prime location and impeccable service, Hotel Milano & Spa provides the perfect base for exploring all that Verona has to offer. For bookings and further details, visit www.hotelmilano.com.

Hotel Veronesi La Torre

Experience the epitome of luxury and refinement at Hotel Veronesi La Torre, within a picturesque park just minutes from Verona's city center. This five-star hotel offers a serene oasis away from the hustle and bustle of the urban landscape, providing guests with a peaceful retreat amidst lush greenery and tranquil surroundings. Accommodations at Hotel Veronesi La Torre range from elegant rooms to lavish suites, each meticulously designed to ensure maximum comfort and relaxation. Guests can indulge in the hotel's exclusive spa, complete with a heated indoor pool, sauna, and steam room, or dine at the onsite restaurant, which serves exquisite Italian cuisine made with locally sourced ingredients. With its emphasis on luxury, wellness, and sustainability, Hotel Veronesi La Torre offers a truly unparalleled experience for discerning travelers. For reservations and more information, visit www.hotelveronesilatorre.com.

2.2 Bed and Breakfasts and Guesthouses

Verona offers visitors a plethora of charming accommodations to enhance their stay. Among the many options, Bed and Breakfasts (B&Bs) and Guesthouses stand out for their personalized service, cozy atmosphere, and often unique touches that provide a memorable experience. In this essay, we delve into five distinct establishments in Verona, each offering its own blend of comfort, character, and hospitality.

La Corte di Giulietta

La Corte di Giulietta captures the essence of romance with its proximity to Juliet's famous balcony. This elegant guesthouse boasts beautifully appointed rooms, each adorned with period furnishings and modern amenities. Prices for lodging vary depending on room selection, ranging from €120 to €250 per night.

Guests at La Corte di Giulietta can enjoy complimentary breakfast served in a picturesque courtyard, complete with freshly baked pastries and local delicacies.

Unique to this guesthouse is the opportunity to arrange private tours of Verona's landmarks, enhancing the cultural experience. For those seeking a truly romantic stay, special packages including champagne and roses can be arranged upon request. Meal prices are not included in the lodging fees but can be enjoyed at the on-site restaurant, offering traditional Italian cuisine with a modern twist. Reservations can be made directly through their official website, where detailed information about room options, rates, and additional services is available. Official Website: (https://www.lacortedigiulietta.com/).

Casa Panvinio

Located just steps away from Verona's Arena, Casa Panvinio offers guests a blend of comfort and convenience in a historic setting. This charming B&B features cozy rooms adorned with antique furnishings and modern amenities, creating a welcoming retreat for travelers. Prices for lodging range from €80 to €180 per night, catering to various budgets and preferences. Guests at Casa Panvinio can start their day with a delicious continental breakfast served in the quaint dining area, featuring freshly brewed coffee and a selection of pastries and fruits. One of the unique features of this B&B is its personalized concierge service, where staff members are readily available to assist with excursion planning, restaurant reservations, and insider tips for exploring Verona. To book a stay at Casa Panvinio, visitors can visit their official website, where detailed descriptions of rooms and amenities are provided, along with the option to make reservations online. Official Website: (https://www.casapanvinio.it/).

Palazzo Victoria

Situated in a meticulously restored 14th-century palace, Palazzo Victoria offers luxury accommodations in the heart of Verona's historic center. This boutique hotel features elegantly appointed rooms and suites, each exuding timeless charm and sophistication. Prices for lodging at Palazzo Victoria start at €250 per night for a classic room and can reach up to €800 per night for a suite. Guests staying at Palazzo Victoria can indulge in a sumptuous buffet breakfast served in the grandeur of the hotel's courtyard, showcasing a selection of Italian pastries, fresh fruits, and gourmet specialties. The hotel's concierge service is available to assist with arranging guided tours, tickets to cultural events, and private transportation, ensuring a seamless experience for guests. Reservations at Palazzo Victoria can be made through their official website, where guests can explore room options, amenities, and special packages available for an unforgettable stay in Verona. Official Website: (https://www.palazzovictoria.com/).

Locanda ai Capitelli

Tucked away in a quiet corner of Verona's historic center, Locanda ai Capitelli offers a peaceful retreat for discerning travelers. This intimate guesthouse features cozy rooms decorated in a rustic style, providing a cozy and inviting ambiance for guests. Prices for lodging at Locanda ai Capitelli range from €70 to €150 per night, making it an affordable option for budget-conscious travelers. Guests at Locanda ai Capitelli can enjoy a continental breakfast served in the charming dining area, featuring freshly baked pastries, artisanal jams, and locally sourced cheeses. The guesthouse offers personalized recommendations for exploring Verona, including hidden gems and off-the-beaten-path attractions. While Locanda ai Capitelli does not have an on-site restaurant, guests can explore nearby trattorias and osterias to savor authentic Italian cuisine. For those looking to unwind after a day of sightseeing, the guesthouse offers a cozy lounge area where guests can relax with a glass of wine and unwind. To book a stay at Locanda ai Capitelli, visitors can visit their official website, where detailed information about room options, rates, and additional services is provided, along with the option to make reservations online. Official Website: (https://www.locanda-aicapitelli.it/).

B&B Verona

Located in a historic building overlooking the Adige River, B&B Verona offers guests a charming retreat in the heart of Verona's historic center. This cozy bed and breakfast feature comfortable rooms decorated in a traditional style, providing a warm and inviting atmosphere for guests. Prices for lodging at B&B Verona range from €60 to €120 per night, catering to various budgets and preferences. Guests at B&B Verona can enjoy a continental breakfast served in the elegant dining area, featuring freshly brewed coffee, pastries, and a selection of homemade jams. The B&B offers personalized concierge service, assisting guests with arranging guided tours, restaurant reservations, and transportation. To book a stay at B&B Verona, visitors can visit their official website, where detailed information about room options, amenities, and rates is provided, along with the option to make reservations online. Official Website:(https://www.bbverona.com/).

2.3 Boutique Hotels and Luxury Resorts

These establishments are not merely places to stay; they are experiences unto themselves, promising a journey through history, art, and unparalleled hospitality. Let us delve into the exquisite world of such establishments, where luxury meets authenticity amidst Verona's timeless beauty.

Hotel Gabbia d'Oro

Steeped in history and elegance, Hotel Gabbia d'Oro offers a truly immersive experience in the heart of Verona's historic center. Housed within a meticulously restored 16th-century palazzo, this boutique hotel exudes old-world charm and sophistication at every turn. Guests can choose from a selection of beautifully appointed rooms and suites, each offering a unique blend of traditional Italian décor and modern comforts. Prices for lodging start at €350 per night for a classic double room. Meal prices at Hotel Gabbia d'Oro's restaurant vary depending on the selection, with an average cost of €70 per person for a three-course meal. To make reservations or learn more about the hotel's offerings, visitors can visit the official website at www.hotelgabbiadoro.com.

Due Torri Hotel

Situated in the heart of Verona's historic center, just steps away from the city's most iconic landmarks, Due Torri Hotel offers a refined blend of luxury and history. Housed within a beautifully restored 14th-century palazzo, this elegant boutique hotel boasts an array of meticulously appointed rooms and suites, each offering breathtaking views of the surrounding cityscape. Prices for lodging start at €400 per night for a deluxe double room. Beyond its luxurious accommodations, Due Torri Hotel offers a wealth of amenities to ensure a memorable stay. Guests can indulge in a range of rejuvenating spa treatments at the hotel's wellness center, or savor gourmet Italian cuisine at the Michelin-starred restaurant, overseen by acclaimed chef Giancarlo Perbellini. For those seeking to explore Verona's cultural heritage, the hotel offers personalized guided tours and exclusive access to local attractions. Meal prices at Due Torri Hotel's restaurant vary depending on the selection, with an average cost of €100 per person for a three-course meal. To make reservations or inquire about availability, visitors can visit the official website at www.hotelduetorri.com.

Bauer Palazzo

Bauer Palazzo offers a tranquil oasis in the heart of Verona's bustling city center. Housed within a meticulously restored 18th-century palazzo, this luxury boutique hotel combines timeless elegance with modern sophistication. Guests can choose from a selection of beautifully appointed rooms and suites, each offering panoramic views of the surrounding cityscape. Prices for lodging start at €350 per night for a classic double room. In addition to its luxurious accommodations, Bauer Palazzo offers a range of amenities to ensure a memorable stay. Guests can unwind with a leisurely swim in the hotel's rooftop pool, or enjoy a relaxing massage at the on-site spa. For those looking to explore Verona's culinary delights, the hotel's restaurant serves up a tantalizing array of Italian and international dishes, crafted with the finest seasonal ingredients. Meal prices at Bauer Palazzo's restaurant vary depending on the selection, with an average cost of €80 per person for a three-course meal. To make reservations or learn more about the hotel's offerings, visitors can visit the official website at www.bauerpalazzo.com.

Byblos Art Hotel Villa Amistà

Tucked away amidst the rolling hills of the Valpolicella wine region, Byblos Art Hotel Villa Amistà offers a serene retreat just a short drive from Verona's city center. Housed within a stunning 15th-century villa, this luxury resort combines old-world charm with contemporary elegance, creating an atmosphere of timeless sophistication. Guests can choose from a selection of beautifully appointed rooms and suites, each featuring unique artwork and luxurious amenities. Prices for lodging start at €500 per night for a classic double room. In addition to its luxurious accommodations, Byblos Art Hotel Villa Amistà offers a wealth of amenities to ensure a memorable stay. Guests can unwind with a leisurely stroll through the hotel's lush gardens, or relax with a glass of fine Italian wine at the elegant bar. For those looking to explore the surrounding area, the hotel provides personalized guided tours of local wineries and cultural landmarks. Meal prices at Byblos Art Hotel Villa Amistà's restaurant vary depending on the selection, with an average cost of €120 per person for a three-course meal. To make reservations or inquire about availability, visitors can visit the official website at www.byblosarthotel.com.

2.4 Apartment Rentals and Vacation Homes

For those looking to truly immerse themselves in the local lifestyle, renting an apartment or vacation home can offer a unique opportunity to live like a local while exploring all that this enchanting city has to offer. From charming apartments nestled in historic neighborhoods to luxurious vacation homes with panoramic views, Verona boasts a plethora of rental options to suit every taste and budget.

Casa Giulietta

Casa Giulietta, located in the heart of Verona's historic center, offers guests the chance to reside in a beautifully restored 17th-century building just a stone's throw away from Juliet's famous balcony. This charming apartment features traditional Venetian decor, with exposed wooden beams and antique furnishings, providing guests with a cozy and authentic living experience. Accommodations at Casa Giulietta range from spacious studios to multi-bedroom apartments, each equipped with modern amenities such as fully equipped kitchens, free Wi-Fi, and air conditioning. Guests can also enjoy access to a private courtyard, perfect for enjoying a morning espresso or evening aperitivo. With its prime location and affordable rates, Casa Giulietta provides the perfect base for exploring all that Verona has to offer. For bookings and more information, visit www.casagiulietta.com.

La Terrazza di

For those seeking a luxurious retreat with breathtaking views of the city, La Terrazza di Verona offers an unparalleled experience. Situated in a historic palazzo overlooking the picturesque rooftops of Verona, this stunning vacation home boasts spacious accommodations and modern amenities designed for comfort and relaxation. Guests can choose from a selection of elegantly furnished apartments, each featuring private terraces or balconies where they can soak in the panoramic vistas of the city below. La Terrazza di Verona also offers a range of special services, including personalized concierge assistance, private chef services, and guided tours of the city's landmarks. Whether enjoying a romantic getaway or a family vacation, guests are sure to create lasting memories at this exquisite retreat. For reservations and further details, visit www.laterrazzadiverona.com.

Casa Bella Vita

For travelers seeking a home away from home in Verona's charming historic district, Casa Bella Vita offers a delightful retreat with all the comforts of modern living. This tastefully appointed vacation home is located just steps away from Verona's main attractions, including the Arena di Verona and Piazza delle Erbe, making it an ideal choice for those looking to explore the city on foot. Accommodations at Casa Bella Vita feature spacious living areas, fully equipped kitchens, and stylish furnishings, providing guests with a comfortable and inviting space to unwind after a day of sightseeing. The rental also includes complimentary Wi-Fi, satellite TV, and air conditioning, ensuring a pleasant stay for all visitors. With its convenient location and affordable rates, Casa Bella Vita is the perfect choice for travelers looking to experience the magic of Verona firsthand. For bookings and additional information, visit www.casabellavita.com.

Palazzo Verita

For a truly immersive experience in the heart of Verona's historic center, Palazzo Verita offers guests the chance to stay in a beautifully restored Renaissance palace dating back to the 16th century. This luxurious vacation rental features elegantly appointed apartments, each showcasing original architectural details such as frescoed ceilings, marble fireplaces, and ornate stucco work. Guests can choose from a variety of accommodations, ranging from intimate studios to spacious suites, all of which are equipped with modern amenities such as fully equipped kitchens, plush bedding, and complimentary toiletries. Palazzo Verita also offers a range of special services, including private chef dinners, guided tours of the city, and in-room spa treatments, ensuring a truly unforgettable stay for discerning travelers. With its unparalleled elegance and historic charm,

Palazzo Verita promises a once-in-a-lifetime experience in the heart of Verona. For reservations and more information, visit www.palazzoverita.com.

2.5 Unique Accommodations: Agriturismo and Vineyard Stays

Agriturismo and Vineyard Stays stand out for their immersive experiences, allowing guests to immerse themselves in the region's culture, cuisine, and natural beauty. In this guide, we explore distinct establishments in Verona, each offering its own blend of rustic charm, hospitality, and unforgettable experiences.

Corte San Mattia Agriturismo

Located amidst the rolling hills of Valpolicella, Corte San Mattia Agriturismo offers guests a tranquil escape surrounded by vineyards and olive groves. This charming agriturismo features cozy rooms and apartments, each boasting traditional décor and modern amenities. Prices for lodging at Corte San Mattia range from €80 to €150 per night, catering to various budgets and preferences. One of the unique features of Corte San Mattia is its farm-to-table restaurant, where guests can savor traditional Veronese cuisine made with ingredients harvested from the estate's gardens. The restaurant also offers wine pairings, allowing guests to experience the perfect marriage of food and wine. To book a stay at Corte San Mattia Agriturismo, visitors can visit their official website, where detailed information about accommodations, activities, and dining options is provided, along with the option to make reservations online. Official Website: (https://www.cortesanmattia.it/en/).

Villa Mosconi Bertani

Villa Mosconi Bertani offers guests a luxurious retreat surrounded by historic vineyards and gardens. This elegant villa features beautifully appointed rooms and suites, each blending classic Italian design with modern comforts. Prices for lodging at Villa Mosconi Bertani start at €250 per night for a classic room and can reach up to €600 per night for a suite. One of the highlights of Villa Mosconi Bertani is its gourmet restaurant, serving exquisite dishes inspired by traditional Veronese cuisine. Guests can dine al fresco on the villa's terrace, overlooking the vineyards and gardens, while enjoying panoramic views of the surrounding countryside. Reservations at Villa Mosconi Bertani can be made through their official website, where guests can explore room options, amenities, and special packages available for an unforgettable stay in Verona. Official Website: (https://www.villamosconibertani.it/en/).

Corte Valpolicella Vineyard

Situated in the picturesque Valpolicella wine region, Corte Valpolicella Vineyard offers guests a unique opportunity to experience life on a working vineyard. This charming agriturismo features rustic-chic accommodations, including rooms and apartments, each offering panoramic views of the surrounding vineyards and countryside. Prices for lodging at Corte Valpolicella Vineyard range from €90 to €200 per night, depending on room size and amenities. One of the unique features of Corte Valpolicella Vineyard is its outdoor pool, surrounded by lush gardens and vineyards, providing the perfect spot to relax and unwind after a day of exploration. The agriturismo also offers bike rentals, allowing guests to explore the scenic countryside at their leisure. To book a stay at Corte Valpolicella Vineyard, visitors can visit their official website, where detailed information about accommodations, activities, and dining options is provided, along with the option to make reservations online. Official Website: (https://www.cortevalpolicella.com/).

Azienda Agricola Monte Tondo

Perched atop the hills overlooking Verona, Azienda Agricola Monte Tondo offers guests a tranquil escape surrounded by vineyards and olive groves. This family-owned winery features charming guest rooms and apartments, each boasting stunning views of the surrounding countryside. Prices for lodging at

Azienda Agricola Monte Tondo range from €70 to €150 per night, catering to various budgets and preferences. Guests at Azienda Agricola Monte Tondo can participate in guided tours of the winery, where they can learn about the winemaking process and sample a selection of the estate's award-winning wines. The winery also offers wine tastings, allowing guests to explore the diverse range of wines produced on the estate. Reservations at Azienda Agricola Monte Tondo can be made through their official website, where detailed information about accommodations, activities, and dining options is provided, along with the option to make reservations online. Official Website:(https://www.montetondo.it/en/).

CHAPTER 3
TRANSPORTATION IN VERONA

3.1 Getting to Verona

Embarking on a journey to Verona offers an exhilarating blend of anticipation and discovery. Whether traversing the skies, railways, or highways, travelers are greeted with a myriad of options to suit their preferences and budgetary considerations. By embracing the convenience of modern transportation and the timeless allure of Italian landscapes, visitors to Verona embark on an unforgettable odyssey filled with enriching experiences and cherished memories.

Air Travel

For travelers seeking swift access to Verona, air travel stands as the most convenient option. Verona Airport, also known as Valerio Catullo Airport (VRN), serves as the primary gateway to the city. Several airlines operate flights to Verona from various international destinations, facilitating seamless connectivity. Among these carriers, prominent names include Lufthansa (https://www.lufthansa.com/), British Airways (https://www.britishairways.com/), Air France (https://www.airfrance.us/), and Ryanair (https://www.ryanair.com/). Each airline offers its unique blend of amenities, schedules, and pricing options, catering to diverse traveler preferences.

Train Travel

Embracing the scenic allure of Italian landscapes, train travel to Verona promises an enchanting experience. Verona Porta Nuova serves as the principal railway station, connecting the city with major domestic and international destinations. Trenitalia, Italy's primary railway operator, offers an extensive network of high-speed and regional trains, facilitating seamless access to Verona from cities like Milan, Venice, Florence, and Rome.

Travelers can book train tickets to Verona through various channels, including the official Trenitalia website (https://www.trenitalia.com/), mobile app, or ticket counters at railway stations. Additionally, alternative rail operators such as Italo provide additional options for travelers seeking flexibility in schedules and amenities. Ticket prices for train journeys to Verona vary based on factors like the class of travel, train type, and advance booking discounts.

Road Travel

Embarking on a road trip to Verona unveils a captivating journey through Italy's picturesque landscapes and quaint towns. The city enjoys excellent road connectivity, making it accessible via well-maintained highways and scenic routes. Travelers opting for road travel can choose between driving their vehicles or utilizing intercity bus services. For those driving to Verona, navigating Italy's road network offers a sense of freedom and flexibility to explore at one's pace. International visitors should familiarize themselves with Italian traffic regulations, including speed limits, tolls, and parking guidelines. Rental car services are readily available at major airports and urban centers, providing travelers with a hassle-free means of transportation.

Alternatively, intercity bus services operated by companies like FlixBus and Marino connect Verona with neighboring cities and European destinations. Travelers can book bus tickets through company websites, mobile apps, or ticket counters at designated terminals. Bus fares to Verona vary based on factors such as distance, class of service, and booking preferences.

3.2 Public Transport: Bus and Metro

Verona's public transport network offers convenient options such as buses, metro, and more. In this comprehensive guide, we delve into the intricacies of navigating Verona's public transportation, including available systems, ticket prices, and effective strategies for getting around.

Bus Services

Verona boasts a well-developed bus network, operated primarily by ATV (Azienda Trasporti Verona). These buses crisscross the city, connecting major landmarks, residential areas, and suburbs. Visitors can easily spot bus stops marked with clear signage displaying route numbers and destinations. With a fleet of modern, comfortable buses equipped with air conditioning, traveling around Verona via bus is both convenient and enjoyable.

Metro System

While Verona doesn't have a traditional metro system like larger cities, it does offer a limited tram service, known as the Verona Metro. The tram lines traverse key areas within the city center, providing an efficient mode of transportation for both locals and tourists. Although the metro network is not as extensive as those in other cities, it serves as a valuable complement to the bus system, particularly for navigating central Verona.

Ticketing and Pricing

Navigating Verona's public transportation system is made simple with the availability of various ticketing options tailored to different travel durations and preferences. Passengers can purchase tickets from authorized vendors, including tobacconists, newsstands, and automated ticket machines located at major bus stops and metro stations. Prices for single journey tickets typically range from €1.30 to €2.50, depending on the distance traveled and the type of service utilized. For travelers planning an extended stay, convenient multi-day passes are available, offering unlimited rides within specified timeframes at competitive rates.

3.3 Taxis and Ride-Sharing Services

Verona offers a range of taxi and ride-sharing services. These services provide visitors with flexible, convenient, and comfortable travel options, ensuring a seamless exploration of the city. In this detailed guide, we delve into the various taxi and ride-sharing companies available in Verona, providing essential information such as locations, contact details, pricing, and tips to enhance your travel experience.

Taxi Services in Verona

Verona's taxi services are an integral part of the city's transportation network, offering reliable and efficient options for visitors who prefer direct and personalized travel.

Radiotaxi Verona

Among the prominent taxi companies in Verona, Radiotaxi Verona stands out. Located at Via del Pontiere 3, this company is renowned for its prompt service and professional drivers. Their official website, www.radiotaxiverona.it, provides comprehensive information on services, rates, and booking options. Generally, taxi fares in Verona start at around €3.50, with additional charges based on distance traveled and time of day.

Taxi & Co.

Another notable company is Taxi & Co., based at Piazzale XXV Aprile, which operates a fleet of well-maintained vehicles catering to both locals and tourists. Their website, www.taxiveronaco.it, allows for easy booking and offers insights into fare structures. Taxis in Verona also offer services for special needs, including vehicles equipped for passengers with disabilities, ensuring inclusive and accessible transportation.

Ride-Sharing Services

In addition to traditional taxis, Verona has embraced modern ride-sharing services, providing visitors with even more flexibility and convenience. One of the leading ride-sharing companies operating in Verona is Uber. Although

Uber's presence in Italy is more limited compared to other countries, it remains a popular choice for many visitors. Uber's app-based platform allows for quick and easy booking, with fare estimates provided before the ride begins, ensuring transparency and peace of mind.

Another popular ride-sharing service in Verona is *Free Now*, formerly known as *mytaxi.* This service offers a seamless blend of traditional taxi convenience and modern technology. Free Now allows users to book rides via their app, *(available on google playstore and applestore),* providing real-time tracking, fare estimates, and cashless payments. Their user-friendly interface and reliable service make them a preferred choice among tech-savvy travelers.

Local Ride-Sharing Companies

Verona also boasts several local ride-sharing companies that cater specifically to the city's unique needs. For instance, *Car Sharing Verona,* located at Via Anfiteatro 10, offers a flexible car rental service designed for short-term use. Their website, www.carsharingverona.it, provides detailed information on membership plans, vehicle availability, and pricing structures. This service is ideal for visitors who prefer the convenience of a private vehicle without the long-term commitment of traditional car rentals.

Enjoy Verona

Furthermore, Enjoy Verona is another noteworthy service, operated by Eni. This company provides a fleet of eco-friendly vehicles available for short-term rentals throughout the city. Their website, www.enjoyverona.it, offers easy booking options and comprehensive details on vehicle locations and usage policies. Enjoy Verona's focus on sustainability makes it an attractive choice for environmentally conscious travelers.

3.4 Renting a Car or Scooter

Exploring the enchanting city of Verona and its surrounding regions is best enjoyed with the freedom and flexibility offered by renting a car or scooter. This guide provides comprehensive insights into renting vehicles in Verona, including details on rental companies, their locations, contact information, websites, and pricing.

Car Rental in Verona

Verona's well-developed infrastructure makes it an ideal city for car rentals, offering visitors the convenience to explore its historical landmarks and picturesque countryside at their own pace. Several reputable car rental companies operate within the city, each providing a range of vehicles to suit different needs and budgets.

Hertz

Hertz is one such renowned company with a strong presence in Verona. Their office is conveniently located at Verona Porta Nuova Railway Station, making it accessible for travelers arriving by train. The Hertz website (www.hertz.com) offers a seamless booking experience, allowing customers to choose from a wide array of vehicles, from compact cars to luxury sedans. Prices for car rentals typically start at around €40 per day for economy models, with additional insurance and GPS options available.

Europcar

Europcar is another prominent name in the car rental industry, with a location near Verona Airport (Valerio Catullo Airport). Europcar's website (www.europcar.com) provides detailed information on available vehicles, pricing, and special offers. Daily rental rates generally begin at approximately €35 for smaller cars, with discounts for longer rental periods.

Avis

Avis, located at Viale del Lavoro, is well-regarded for its extensive fleet and customer service. Visitors can book their rentals through the Avis website (www.avis.com), where they can explore various vehicle categories, from budget-friendly options to premium models. Prices for a standard car rental with Avis usually start at around €38 per day.

Sixt

Sixt, found at Verona Porta Nuova Railway Station, offers competitive pricing and a diverse range of vehicles. Their user-friendly website (www.sixt.com) allows for easy online bookings, providing transparency on costs and rental conditions. Rates for Sixt rentals typically start at €37 per day for economy cars, with luxury options also available.

Budget Car Rental

Budget Car Rental, located on Via Torricelli, is another excellent choice for visitors looking for cost-effective options. Their website (www.budget.com) lists a variety of rental vehicles, ensuring that travelers can find the perfect car to suit their needs. Prices for Budget rentals start at around €33 per day, making it an attractive option for budget-conscious visitors.

Scooter Rental in Verona

For those who prefer a more adventurous and nimble way to explore Verona, renting a scooter offers an exciting alternative. Scooters are perfect for navigating the narrow streets of the historic city center and accessing scenic viewpoints with ease. Cooltra is a popular scooter rental company in Verona, known for its extensive fleet and excellent service. Located on Corso Porta Nuova, Cooltra provides a variety of scooters to choose from, including 50cc and 125cc models. Their website (www.cooltra.com) allows for convenient online bookings, with prices starting at around €30 per day. Cooltra also offers additional equipment such as helmets and insurance packages.

Verona Rent

Verona Rent, situated near Piazza Bra, is another reputable company offering scooter rentals. Visitors can explore their offerings on the Verona Rent website (www.veronarent.com), which details the various scooter models available for hire. Rental prices typically begin at €28 per day, with discounts for multi-day rentals.

Bikys

Bikys, located on Via IV Novembre, provides a range of scooters perfect for exploring both the city and the surrounding countryside. Their website (www.bikys.it) features an easy-to-navigate booking system, with daily rental rates starting at approximately €25. Bikys also offers guided scooter tours for those looking to discover Verona's hidden gems with the help of a local guide.

Motorent Verona

Motorent Verona, positioned near Verona Porta Vescovo Railway Station, is well-known for its customer-friendly service and well-maintained scooters. Through their website (www.motorentverona.com), visitors can browse and book scooters online, with prices starting at around €27 per day. Motorent Verona also provides helmets and locks as part of the rental package.

Scooternoleggio

Scooternoleggio, located on Via del Pontiere, offers a variety of scooters suitable for different riding preferences. Their website (www.scooternoleggio.com) provides comprehensive information on available models and pricing, with daily rates beginning at €26. Scooternoleggio also includes essential accessories like helmets and maps to ensure a safe and enjoyable riding experience.

3.5 Exploring on Foot: Walking Tours and Bike Rentals

Verona offers a treasure trove of sights and experiences. This guide provides an in-depth look at exploring Verona on foot and renting bikes, complete with detailed information about walking tours, bike rental companies, and essential tips for visitors.

Walking Tours in Verona

Verona's compact city center, rich in history and architectural wonders, makes it an ideal destination for walking tours. Walking allows visitors to immerse themselves fully in the city's ambiance, offering a slower, more intimate look at its famed attractions Many guided walking tours are available, catering to various interests. For instance, you can join a historical tour that covers the city's Roman origins, medieval structures, and Renaissance influences. Such tours typically include visits to iconic sites like the Arena di Verona, Piazza delle Erbe, and Juliet's House. For literary enthusiasts, there are tours dedicated to Shakespeare's "Romeo and Juliet," providing insights into the legendary love story that Verona famously inspired.

These tours are usually led by knowledgeable local guides who share fascinating stories and lesser-known facts about Verona's history and culture. Prices for walking tours vary depending on their duration and the inclusivity of the itinerary, but you can generally expect to pay between €20 to €50 per person. Some companies also offer themed tours, such as food and wine tours, which combine sightseeing with culinary delights, offering tastings of local delicacies and visits to traditional eateries.

Bike Rentals in Verona

For those who prefer a bit more speed while exploring, bike rentals are a fantastic option. Biking through Verona allows you to cover more ground while still maintaining a close connection to the city's sights and sounds. Several bike rental companies in Verona cater to tourists, each offering various services and pricing to fit different needs.

Verona Bike Rental

Located near the Porta Nuova train station, is a popular choice for many visitors. They offer a wide range of bicycles, from standard city bikes to electric bikes for those who prefer a less strenuous ride. Their prices start at around €15 per day for a standard bike and can go up to €30 per day for an electric bike. You can contact them via their website (http://veronabikerental.com) or visit their store at Corso Porta Nuova, 93, 37122 Verona.

Bike Verona

Another reputable company is Bike Verona, situated near the historic city center. They offer both hourly and daily rentals, with prices starting at €10 for two hours or €20 for a full day. Their website, (http://bikeverona.it), provides detailed information on bike models and booking options. Their shop is conveniently located at Via Ponte Pietra, 3, 37121 Verona, making it easy to pick up and drop off bikes.

Verona Rent & Ride

Verona Rent & Ride offers a unique combination of bike rentals and guided bike tours. Located at Via Roma, 22, 37121 Verona, this company provides bikes for €18 per day. They also organize bike tours around the city and into the countryside, blending sightseeing with an active adventure. More details can be found on their website (http://veronarentandride.com).

Amici di Bici: Amici di Bici, another excellent option, focuses on providing eco-friendly electric bikes. Their shop is located at Via IV Novembre, 4, 37126 Verona. They offer daily rentals starting at €25 and have various packages for longer rentals. Their website, (http://amicidibici.it), includes a booking platform and customer reviews to help you choose the right bike for your needs.

Ciclofficina Verona: Ciclofficina Verona, located at Via Leoncino, 21, 37122 Verona, offers both rentals and repairs, making it a great option if you're planning an extended stay. Their rental rates are competitive, starting at €12 per day for a standard bike. They also provide maps and suggested routes to help you explore Verona and its surroundings. Visit their website (http://ciclofficinaverona.it) for more information.

Essential Tips for Visitors: When planning to explore Verona on foot or by bike, it's essential to consider a few practical tips to make your experience smooth and enjoyable. Firstly, Verona's weather can be quite varied, so it's wise to check the forecast and dress appropriately. Comfortable walking shoes are a must if you're joining a walking tour, as the city's cobblestone streets can be tough on your feet. For biking, lightweight clothing and a helmet (which is often included in the rental) will ensure a safer ride. Additionally, Verona is a relatively safe city, but like any tourist destination, it's important to stay aware of your surroundings and secure your belongings. Most bike rental companies provide locks, and it's a good practice to use them whenever you park your bike.

Understanding local traffic rules is also crucial when biking. Verona's city center has many pedestrian-only zones, and while bikes are generally allowed, it's important to respect pedestrian spaces and be mindful of local regulations. Finally, don't forget to take advantage of Verona's public fountains scattered throughout the city. They provide fresh drinking water, perfect for refilling your bottle and staying hydrated, especially during the warmer months.

CHAPTER 4
TOP 10 HIDDEN GEM ATTRACTIONS

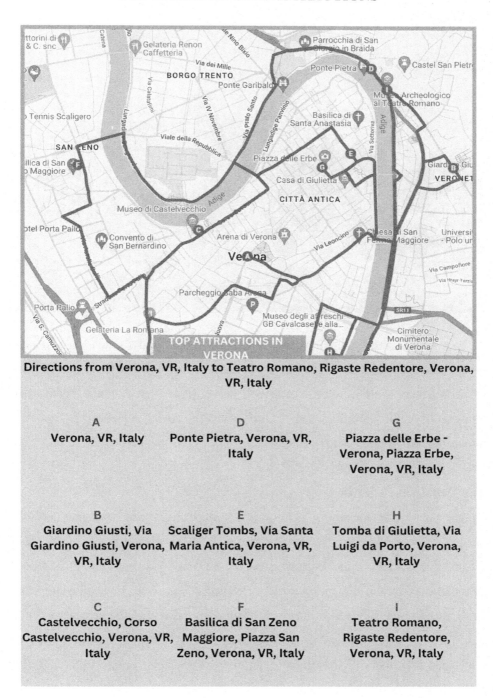

Directions from Verona, VR, Italy to Teatro Romano, Rigaste Redentore, Verona, VR, Italy

A Verona, VR, Italy	D Ponte Pietra, Verona, VR, Italy	G Piazza delle Erbe - Verona, Piazza Erbe, Verona, VR, Italy
B Giardino Giusti, Via Giardino Giusti, Verona, VR, Italy	E Scaliger Tombs, Via Santa Maria Antica, Verona, VR, Italy	H Tomba di Giulietta, Via Luigi da Porto, Verona, VR, Italy
C Castelvecchio, Corso Castelvecchio, Verona, VR, Italy	F Basilica di San Zeno Maggiore, Piazza San Zeno, Verona, VR, Italy	I Teatro Romano, Rigaste Redentore, Verona, VR, Italy

4.1 Giardino Giusti

A visit to Giardino Giusti promises an immersion into Renaissance beauty, serene landscapes, and an array of captivating attractions that leave an indelible mark on every visitor. This session will delve into five remarkable features of Giardino Giusti, detailing their significance, location, accessibility, and the unparalleled experiences they offer.

The Renaissance Garden

At the heart of Giardino Giusti is its Renaissance garden, a meticulously designed landscape that transports visitors back to the elegance of the 16th century. Located on the eastern side of Verona, Giardino Giusti is easily accessible by public transportation or a leisurely walk from the city center. The garden's entrance fee is modest, often around 10 euros, which grants access to a world of historical splendor. The Renaissance garden is a masterpiece of landscape architecture, showcasing symmetrical designs, ornate fountains, and meticulously trimmed hedges. Walking through this garden, visitors are enveloped by the scent of blooming flowers and the gentle sound of water trickling from the fountains. The garden's layout is a reflection of the Renaissance ideals of order and beauty, making it a perfect spot for photography, sketching, or simply basking in the tranquil ambiance.

The Avenue of Cypress Trees

One of the most iconic features of Giardino Giusti is the Avenue of Cypress Trees, a long, elegant pathway flanked by towering cypress trees that lead up to a panoramic terrace. This avenue is located centrally within the garden and can be reached by following the main paths that wind through the estate. The towering cypress trees, which have stood for centuries, create a dramatic and serene walkway that culminates in a breathtaking view of Verona. This path not only offers a picturesque setting but also serves as a natural corridor that guides visitors through different sections of the garden. Walking along this avenue, one can feel the weight of history and the timeless beauty that has been preserved over the years.

The Labyrinth

Tucked away in a secluded part of Giardino Giusti is the labyrinth, a charming and playful feature that invites visitors to lose themselves in its winding paths. Located towards the back of the garden, the labyrinth is a hidden gem that often surprises and delights those who discover it. The labyrinth, made from neatly trimmed hedges, offers a fun and interactive experience for visitors of all ages. Navigating its twists and turns provides a sense of adventure and curiosity, reminiscent of the historical garden mazes that were popular in European estates. The design of the labyrinth encourages exploration and provides a whimsical contrast to the more formal sections of the garden.

The Grottoes and Fountains

Giardino Giusti is also renowned for its grottoes and fountains, which add an element of mystery and wonder to the garden. These features are dispersed throughout the garden, often hidden within the lush greenery, waiting to be discovered by curious visitors. The grottoes, constructed from natural rock formations, provide cool, shaded retreats that contrast with the open, sunlit areas of the garden. These grottoes were designed to mimic natural caves, offering a sense of seclusion and tranquility. Historically, grottoes in Renaissance gardens were symbols of the natural world and often served as places for contemplation and relaxation.

The Belvedere and the Tower

Perched at the highest point of Giardino Giusti is the Belvedere and its adjacent tower, offering unparalleled views of the garden and the city of Verona. This area is accessed by climbing a series of steps that wind through the garden, leading visitors to the top where the effort is rewarded with breathtaking vistas. The Belvedere provides a panoramic view that captures the essence of Verona's beauty, from its medieval architecture to its picturesque landscapes. This spot is ideal for photography, sketching, or simply soaking in the view. The tower, which can be ascended for an even higher vantage point, offers a 360-degree view that is particularly stunning at sunset.

4.2 Castelvecchio Museum

The Castelvecchio Museum, In the heart of Verona, Italy, is a treasure trove of art, history, and culture. This museum, housed in a magnificent medieval castle, offers visitors a unique glimpse into Verona's rich past and artistic heritage. Beyond its well-known attractions, the museum harbors several hidden gems that make it a must-visit destination for any traveler seeking an authentic and enriching experience. Let's delve into some of these remarkable spots within the Castelvecchio Museum that promise to captivate and inspire.

The Medieval Castle Itself

The Castelvecchio Museum is situated in the iconic Castelvecchio Castle, a structure that exudes historical grandeur. Located on Corso Castelvecchio, it is easily accessible by foot from Verona's city center or via public transportation. The castle, built in the 14th century by the powerful Scaliger dynasty, served as a fortress and residence, reflecting the medieval architecture and defensive strategies of the era.

The Ezzelino Tower

One of the less frequented but equally impressive parts of the Castelvecchio Museum is the Ezzelino Tower. This tower, accessible from within the castle, offers a panoramic view of Verona that is simply unparalleled. Climbing the tower's steep stairs is well worth the effort, as the top rewards visitors with a stunning vista of the city's red-tiled roofs, winding streets, and historic landmarks. The Ezzelino Tower is not just a viewpoint but also a historical artifact in its own right. Named after the notorious tyrant Ezzelino III da Romano, the tower stands as a testament to Verona's turbulent past. From this vantage point, one can appreciate the strategic significance of Castelvecchio's location and gain a deeper understanding of the city's medieval urban planning. There is no additional fee to access the tower, making it a hidden gem within the museum that offers both visual delight and historical insight.

The Art Collection

While Castelvecchio is renowned for its architectural splendor, its extensive art collection is a treasure trove waiting to be explored. The museum's galleries house an impressive array of artworks spanning from the medieval period to the Renaissance. Notable pieces include works by Pisanello, Andrea Mantegna, and Giovanni Bellini. These masterpieces are housed in elegantly designed rooms that enhance their visual impact. The careful curation and display allow visitors to experience the evolution of artistic styles and techniques over centuries. The art collection is particularly significant because it provides a comprehensive overview of the region's artistic heritage. Each piece tells a story, offering insights into the cultural and social contexts of its time.

The Courtyard of the Scaligeri

Hidden within the fortress walls is the Courtyard of the Scaligeri, a serene and picturesque spot that offers a tranquil escape from the bustling city. This courtyard, adorned with sculptures and lush greenery, provides a peaceful setting where visitors can relax and reflect on their museum experience. The Courtyard of the Scaligeri is particularly enchanting because it combines natural beauty with historical artifacts. The carefully landscaped garden is dotted with statues and remnants of the past, creating a harmonious blend of art and nature. It is an ideal place to take a leisurely stroll, sit on a bench, and absorb the tranquil ambiance.

The Chapel of the Holy Cross

Another lesser-known but profoundly moving part of the Castelvecchio Museum is the Chapel of the Holy Cross. This chapel, located within the castle complex, is a place of spiritual and artistic significance. Adorned with exquisite frescoes and religious artifacts, the chapel offers a glimpse into the religious life of medieval Verona. The Chapel of the Holy Cross is an intimate space that exudes a sense of reverence and tranquility. The frescoes, depicting scenes from the life of Christ and various saints, are masterfully executed and have been meticulously preserved. These artworks provide insight into the devotional practices and artistic expressions of the time.

Practical Information for Visitors

The museum offers guided tours in multiple languages, which can greatly enhance the visitor experience by providing expert insights into the history and art of the castle. For those interested in a more in-depth exploration, audio guides are also available for a small fee. These guides offer detailed commentary on the museum's highlights and hidden gems, allowing visitors to appreciate the rich tapestry of history and culture at their own pace. The museum is easily accessible by public transportation, with several bus lines stopping nearby. For those driving, there are parking facilities within walking distance. Additionally, the museum is wheelchair accessible, ensuring that all visitors can enjoy its wonders.

4.3 Ponte Pietra

Ponte Pietra is a captivating location that offers visitors a blend of rich history, cultural significance, and stunning vistas. This ancient Roman arch bridge spans the Adige River and connects various attractions that are often overlooked by the casual tourist. Here, we delve into must-see hidden gems near Ponte Pietra that promise an unforgettable experience.

Teatro Romano

The Teatro Romano, or Roman Theatre, is a marvel of ancient architecture located just a short stroll from Ponte Pietra. Built in the 1st century BC, this theatre once held thousands of spectators and still exudes a sense of grandeur. Visitors can explore the well-preserved remains, including the stage, seating areas, and backstage rooms. The site also houses an archaeological museum, showcasing artifacts from Verona's Roman past. The theatre often hosts cultural events and performances, bringing ancient history to life in a modern context. Entrance fees are minimal, typically around 4-6 euros, making it an accessible adventure for history enthusiasts.

Castel San Pietro

Perched atop a hill overlooking Ponte Pietra and the Adige River, Castel San Pietro offers some of the most breathtaking views in Verona. This fortress dates back to the 14th century, although the hill itself has been inhabited since ancient times. Reaching Castel San Pietro involves a scenic climb or a quick funicular ride, both of which provide unique perspectives of the city. Once at the top, visitors can wander through the castle ruins and enjoy panoramic vistas of Verona's historic center. The site is especially stunning at sunset, making it a perfect spot for photography and relaxation. Entrance to the castle grounds is free, though the funicular ride has a small fee.

Giardino Giusti

Giardino Giusti, an exquisite Renaissance garden, is a hidden oasis of tranquility just a short walk from Ponte Pietra. Created in the 16th century by the Giusti family, the garden is renowned for its manicured lawns, intricate hedges, and statues. It also features a labyrinth and a grotto, adding to its charm. The garden offers a serene escape from the city's hustle and bustle, providing a space for contemplation and leisurely strolls. Visitors can climb to the garden's upper terraces for stunning views of Verona. An entry fee of around 10 euros is required, which is well worth it for the beauty and peace the garden provides.

Duomo di Verona

The Duomo di Verona, or Verona Cathedral, is an architectural gem located near Ponte Pietra. This Romanesque cathedral, built in the 12th century, is dedicated to Santa Maria Matricolare. Its façade is adorned with intricate sculptures and a majestic rose window. Inside, visitors can admire stunning frescoes, marble columns, and the grand altar. The cathedral complex also includes a beautiful cloister and a small museum showcasing religious artifacts. The Duomo is a place of profound spiritual and historical significance, offering a glimpse into Verona's religious heritage. Entrance to the cathedral is free, though a small fee may apply for the museum.

Sant'Anastasia

Sant'Anastasia, the largest church in Verona, is another must-visit site near Ponte Pietra. This Gothic masterpiece, constructed between the 13th and 15th centuries, is renowned for its impressive architecture and artistic treasures. The church's interior is adorned with beautiful frescoes, including the famous Pisanello's fresco of St. George and the Princess. Visitors can also marvel at the intricately carved wooden choir stalls and the magnificent altar. Sant'Anastasia's grandeur and artistic heritage make it a captivating destination for art lovers and history buffs alike. A small entry fee, usually around 3 euros, helps preserve this historic site.

4.4 Scaliger Tombs

Scaliger Tombs, an extraordinary ensemble of Gothic funerary monuments dedicated to the illustrious Scaliger family. These tombs, often overlooked by the casual tourist, stand as a testament to Verona's medieval heritage and artistic grandeur. This guide explores significant features of the Scaliger Tombs, detailing their location, accessibility, historical significance, and the unique experiences they offer to visitors.

The Magnificent Can Signorio Tomb

One of the most striking tombs within the Scaliger Tombs complex is the Can Signorio Tomb, dedicated to Cansignorio della Scala, a prominent member of the Scaliger family who ruled Verona in the 14th century. Located in the heart of Verona, the Scaliger Tombs can be found adjacent to the Church of Santa Maria Antica, near Piazza dei Signori. The tomb complex is easily accessible by foot from the city center or by public transport, with a small entry fee that helps maintain the preservation of these historical monuments. The Can Signorio Tomb is an exquisite example of Gothic architecture, characterized by its intricate carvings, soaring spires, and elaborate sculptures. The tomb is elevated on a pedestal, surrounded by an ornate wrought-iron fence adorned with symbols of the Scala family. Visitors are often struck by the detailed craftsmanship, which includes statues of knights, angels, and the Virgin Mary, all meticulously carved from marble. The tomb's design reflects the wealth and power of the Scaliger family, showcasing their influence and artistic patronage.

The Elegant Mastino II Tomb

Another notable feature of the Scaliger Tombs is the Mastino II Tomb, dedicated to Mastino II della Scala, who was one of the most powerful rulers of Verona. The tomb is located within the same complex, easily accessible once you enter the Scaliger Tombs site. The entry fee to the complex includes access to all the tombs, making it convenient for visitors to explore the entire ensemble. The Mastino II Tomb is distinguished by its elegant design and the remarkable use of Gothic motifs. It is slightly less grandiose than the Can Signorio Tomb but no less impressive. The tomb is adorned with statues of warriors and religious figures, highlighting the dual themes of power and piety that characterized the Scaliger rulers. The canopy above the tomb is particularly noteworthy, featuring intricate stone lacework that exemplifies the Gothic style.

The Artistic Cangrande I Tomb

The Cangrande I Tomb, dedicated to the esteemed ruler Cangrande I della Scala, is one of the most artistically significant monuments within the Scaliger Tombs complex. Cangrande I was known for his military prowess and his patronage of the arts, making his tomb a reflection of both his achievements and his love for culture. The tomb is located near the entrance of the complex, easily identifiable by its elaborate design and prominent placement. The tomb is a masterpiece of Gothic art, featuring a life-sized equestrian statue of Cangrande I, symbolizing his strength and leadership. The statue is placed atop a sarcophagus, which is richly decorated with reliefs depicting scenes from his life and allegorical figures. The canopy above the tomb is adorned with delicate carvings and pinnacles, creating a visually stunning tribute to one of Verona's most revered leaders.

The Peaceful Giovanni della Scala Tomb

Located within the Scaliger Tombs complex is the Giovanni della Scala Tomb, dedicated to Giovanni della Scala, a lesser-known but equally significant member of the Scaliger family. The tomb is situated in a quieter part of the complex, providing a serene and contemplative space for visitors. Access to the tomb is included in the general entry fee, allowing for an unhurried exploration of this peaceful monument. The Giovanni della Scala Tomb is characterized by its understated elegance and harmonious design. Unlike the more elaborate tombs of his relatives, Giovanni's tomb features simpler lines and a focus on spiritual themes. The sarcophagus is adorned with religious symbols and inscriptions, reflecting Giovanni's piety and devotion. The surrounding area is beautifully landscaped, with flowers and greenery enhancing the tranquil atmosphere.

The Historical Arche Scaligere Museum

Completing the exploration of the Scaliger Tombs is the Arche Scaligere Museum, an essential destination for those interested in the historical and cultural context of the monuments. The museum is located adjacent to the tombs, providing easy access for visitors who wish to delve deeper into the history of the Scaliger family and their architectural achievements. The museum houses a collection of artifacts, documents, and exhibits related to the Scaliger dynasty, offering valuable insights into their rule and their contributions to Verona's development. Among the exhibits are detailed models of the tombs, historical maps, and artistic renderings, providing a comprehensive overview of the Gothic era in Verona. The museum also features multimedia displays that bring the history to life, making it an engaging experience for visitors of all ages.

4.5 Basilica di San Zeno Maggiore

Basilica di San Zeno Maggiore stands as a testament to centuries of history, art, and spirituality. Often overshadowed by Verona's more famous attractions, this basilica is a hidden gem that offers a rich and immersive experience for those who seek to uncover its treasures. With its stunning architecture, historical significance, and serene atmosphere, the Basilica di San Zeno Maggiore is a must-visit for any traveler. Let's delve into the top attractions within this magnificent basilica that make it a unique and captivating destination.

The Romanesque Architecture
Located in the western part of Verona, the Basilica di San Zeno Maggiore is easily accessible by a short walk from the city center or by public transportation. As you approach the basilica, the first thing that strikes you is its impressive Romanesque architecture. Constructed between the 9th and 12th centuries, the

basilica is a masterpiece of design, characterized by its harmonious proportions, robust structure, and intricate details. The façade of the basilica is adorned with ornate carvings and a striking rose window, known as the "Wheel of Fortune." This window, created by the renowned sculptor Brioloto, is a visual delight and a symbol of the cyclical nature of life. The main entrance is flanked by two majestic bronze doors, each panel depicting biblical scenes with exquisite craftsmanship. These doors, crafted by the Veronese artist Master Nicolò, are a marvel to behold and offer a glimpse into the artistic heritage of the region.

The Triptych of San Zeno

One of the most significant attractions within the Basilica di San Zeno Maggiore is the renowned Triptych of San Zeno. This altarpiece, created by the early Renaissance painter Andrea Mantegna, is a masterpiece that captures the viewer's imagination with its vibrant colors, intricate details, and profound symbolism. The triptych is located in the main altar area and consists of three panels depicting the Madonna and Child surrounded by saints and angels. Mantegna's use of perspective, his meticulous attention to detail, and the lifelike expressions of the figures make this work a pinnacle of Renaissance art. The central panel, featuring the serene and regal Madonna, is particularly striking and draws visitors into a contemplative state.

The Crypt of San Zeno

Beneath the main altar lies the crypt of San Zeno, a sacred and atmospheric space that offers a journey into the past. The crypt is dedicated to Saint Zeno, the patron saint of Verona, whose relics are housed here. Saint Zeno, an African-born bishop of Verona in the 4th century, is venerated for his piety and miracles. The crypt, with its low vaulted ceilings and ancient columns, exudes a sense of mystery and reverence. It is here that visitors can see the beautifully decorated sarcophagus of Saint Zeno, surrounded by frescoes that depict scenes from his life. The serene and contemplative atmosphere of the crypt invites

56

visitors to reflect on the enduring legacy of Saint Zeno and the deep spiritual roots of Verona.

The Cloister

Adjacent to the basilica is the Cloister of San Zeno, a hidden gem that offers a tranquil retreat from the hustle and bustle of modern life. The cloister, built in the 12th century, is a beautiful example of Romanesque architecture, featuring elegant arches, stone columns, and a peaceful garden. Walking through the cloister, visitors can enjoy the serene ambiance and admire the harmonious design. The central garden, with its lush greenery and fragrant flowers, is a perfect place to sit and reflect. The cloister also houses a small museum with artifacts and historical exhibits that provide further insight into the basilica's history and the monastic life of the past.

The Frescoes

The interior of the Basilica di San Zeno Maggiore is adorned with a stunning array of frescoes that transform the walls into a gallery of sacred art. These frescoes, dating from the 12th to the 15th centuries, depict scenes from the Bible, the lives of saints, and various religious motifs. Each fresco is a work of art, showcasing the skill and devotion of the artists who created them. One of the most notable frescoes is the "Coronation of the Virgin," located in the apse. This masterpiece, painted by the school of Altichiero da Zevio, captures the divine moment with vivid colors and dynamic composition. The figures, rendered with delicate detail and expressive gestures, seem to come to life on the walls of the basilica.

4.6 Piazza delle Erbe Market

Piazza delle Erbe is more than just a marketplace; it's a vibrant center teeming with history, culture, and enchanting sights. While tourists often flock to its stalls and admire its lively atmosphere, the surrounding area harbors several hidden gems that enrich any visit to this storied square. Here, we explore captivating attractions around Piazza delle Erbe that promise to enhance your experience of Verona.

Torre dei Lamberti

Standing tall over Piazza delle Erbe, Torre dei Lamberti offers an unparalleled panoramic view of Verona. This medieval tower, originally constructed in 1172 and subsequently expanded, soars to a height of 84 meters. Visitors can reach the top via a combination of elevator and stairs, with a modest entry fee granting access to this lofty perch. The view from Torre dei Lamberti is nothing short of spectacular, providing a bird's-eye perspective of the city's historic rooftops, the Adige River, and distant hills. The tower's clock and bells add a charming touch to its historical significance, making it a must-visit for those keen on capturing the essence of Verona from above.

Casa di Giulietta

A short walk from Piazza delle Erbe brings you to Casa di Giulietta, the legendary home of Shakespeare's Juliet. This 13th-century house, believed to have inspired the setting for the famous balcony scene in "Romeo and Juliet," is a haven for romantics and literature enthusiasts. Visitors can explore the courtyard and gaze upon the iconic balcony, as well as leave messages of love on the walls. The interior of the house, which requires a small entry fee, offers a glimpse into Verona's medieval past with period furnishings and historical exhibits. For those seeking a deeper connection to one of the world's most famous love stories, Casa di Giulietta is an enchanting stop.

Palazzo Maffei

Dominating the western side of Piazza delle Erbe, Palazzo Maffei is an architectural masterpiece that blends Baroque opulence with classical elegance. Constructed in the 17th century, this palazzo boasts a striking façade adorned with statues of Greek gods. Inside, visitors can explore a rich collection of art and antiques, as well as enjoy temporary exhibitions that showcase various aspects of Verona's cultural heritage. The palazzo's grand staircase and ornate rooms reflect the wealth and sophistication of its historical owners. A visit to Palazzo Maffei, often included in a combined ticket with other local attractions, offers a luxurious journey into Verona's artistic and architectural legacy.

Piazza dei Signori

Just a stone's throw from Piazza delle Erbe lies Piazza dei Signori, a quieter but equally captivating square known for its historical and political significance. Surrounded by important buildings such as the Palazzo della Ragione, the Loggia del Consiglio, and the Arche Scaligere, this square has been a center of power and governance since medieval times. The statue of Dante Alighieri, who spent time in Verona, presides over the square, adding a literary connection to its grandeur. Visitors can soak in the ambiance, admire the architecture, and explore the various palazzi that now house museums, galleries, and municipal offices. The timeless elegance of Piazza dei Signori offers a peaceful contrast to the bustling market of Piazza delle Erbe.

Chiesa di Santa Maria Antica

Tucked away near Piazza dei Signori, the Chiesa di Santa Maria Antica is a hidden gem of religious and architectural significance. This small but historically rich church dates back to the 7th century and is closely associated with the powerful Scaliger family, whose Gothic funerary monuments, the Arche Scaligere, stand just outside. Inside, visitors can find a serene and intimate atmosphere, with Romanesque and Gothic elements blending harmoniously. The church's simplicity and historical importance provide a poignant reminder of Verona's medieval past. Admission is free, making it an accessible and contemplative stop for those exploring the city's hidden corners.

4.7 Roman Theater and Archaeological Museum

Roman Theater and Archaeological Museum stand out as a hidden gem, often overshadowed by more famous sites but equally deserving of admiration. Nestled on the banks of the Adige River, these attractions offer a captivating journey through time, revealing the rich tapestry of Verona's ancient past. This guide delves into compelling features of the Roman Theater and Archaeological Museum, exploring their significance, location, accessibility, and the unique experiences they offer.

The Magnificent Roman Theater

The Roman Theater in Verona, an architectural marvel from the 1st century BC, serves as the centerpiece of this historical site. Located on the northern side of the city, the theater is easily accessible by a scenic walk along the Adige River or a short ride on public transportation. The entrance fee, which is modest, covers access to both the theater and the Archaeological Museum, making it a worthwhile investment for any history enthusiast. The Roman Theater is a

61

testament to the engineering prowess of ancient Rome. Built into the hillside, it offers stunning views of the surrounding landscape and the city. Visitors can explore the well-preserved seating areas, the stage, and the orchestra pit, gaining insight into the social and cultural life of ancient Verona. The theater's acoustics are remarkable, and during the summer, it becomes a venue for performances and events, allowing visitors to experience the magic of ancient drama in its original setting.

The Archaeological Museum's Rich Collections

Adjacent to the Roman Theater is the Archaeological Museum, housed in the former convent of San Girolamo. The museum, which is included in the theater's entrance fee, provides a comprehensive overview of Verona's ancient history through its extensive collections of artifacts. The museum is located just a short climb up the hill from the theater, offering an additional layer of exploration for visitors. The Archaeological Museum boasts an impressive array of Roman artifacts, including statues, mosaics, inscriptions, and everyday objects. Each exhibit tells a story of life in ancient Verona, from the grandeur of public buildings to the intimacy of private homes. Highlights include the beautifully preserved mosaics depicting mythological scenes and the finely crafted statues that once adorned the city's temples and public spaces.

The Panoramic Terrace

One of the most breathtaking features of the Roman Theater and Archaeological Museum complex is the panoramic terrace. Located at the top of the hill, this terrace offers a stunning view of Verona and the Adige River, providing a perfect backdrop for photos and moments of reflection. The terrace is easily accessible from the museum, with a series of well-maintained paths and steps leading the way. The panoramic terrace offers a unique perspective on Verona, allowing visitors to appreciate the city's layout and its historical landmarks from above. On a clear day, the view extends to the distant hills and mountains, creating a picturesque scene that captures the essence of Verona's natural beauty. The terrace is a popular spot for visitors to relax and take in the scenery after exploring the theater and museum.

The Hidden Gem of the Cloister

Within the Archaeological Museum, visitors will find the hidden gem of the cloister, a tranquil and beautifully preserved space that once belonged to the convent of San Girolamo. This cloister, often overlooked by hurried visitors, provides a peaceful retreat and a glimpse into the monastic life that once thrived here. The cloister is located within the museum complex, easily accessible as part of the museum tour. The cloister's architecture is a blend of Romanesque and Gothic styles, with elegant arches and columns framing a central courtyard. The space is adorned with ancient stone carvings and inscriptions, adding to its historical ambiance. Visitors can stroll through the cloister, taking in the serene atmosphere and appreciating the detailed craftsmanship that has been preserved over the centuries.

The Engaging Educational Workshops

The Roman Theater and Archaeological Museum also offer a range of educational workshops and activities designed to engage visitors of all ages. These workshops, often included in the entry fee or available for a small additional cost, provide hands-on learning experiences that bring Verona's ancient history to life. The workshops are held in various locations within the museum and theater complex, making them easily accessible to all visitors. One popular workshop focuses on Roman mosaic-making, allowing participants to create their own miniature mosaics using traditional techniques and materials. Another workshop delves into ancient Roman theater, where visitors can learn about the art of acting and stagecraft in Roman times, culminating in a short performance in the historic theater. These interactive experiences provide a deeper understanding of the daily life, art, and culture of ancient Verona.

4.8 Juliet's Tomb

Juliet's Tomb stands as a poignant testament to love, tragedy, and the enduring power of Shakespearean romance. While many visitors flock to Juliet's House to pay homage to the iconic balcony and love story, Juliet's Tomb often remains a hidden gem waiting to be discovered. Yet, beneath the surface lies a site of historical and cultural significance that beckons travelers to explore its mysteries. Let's embark on a journey to uncover the top attractions within Juliet's Tomb and understand why it is a must-visit destination in Verona.

The Legend of Romeo and Juliet

Juliet's Tomb is steeped in the legend of Shakespeare's tragic lovers, Romeo and Juliet, whose fateful romance captivates hearts around the world. According to popular belief, the tomb housed the remains of Juliet Capulet, the fictional heroine of Shakespeare's play, and served as the backdrop for the climactic scene of their untimely demise. Visitors to Juliet's Tomb can immerse themselves in the timeless tale of love and loss as they stand before the sarcophagus that purportedly held Juliet's body. While the historical veracity of the legend is debated, the emotional resonance of Romeo and Juliet's story endures, drawing visitors to pay their respects and ponder the mysteries of love and destiny.

The Crypt of San Francesco al Corso

Beyond its association with Romeo and Juliet, Juliet's Tomb is housed within the tranquil confines of the crypt of San Francesco al Corso. This sacred space, adorned with ancient frescoes and dimly lit by flickering candlelight, offers a sanctuary of serenity amidst the bustling city. Visitors to the crypt can explore its hallowed halls and reflect on the passage of time and the fragility of life. The peaceful ambiance invites contemplation and introspection, allowing travelers to connect with the spiritual essence of the site and find solace in its quietude.

Practical Information for Visitors

Juliet's Tomb is open to visitors during regular church hours, which may vary depending on the day of the week and any special events or services. It is advisable to check the church's schedule in advance to plan your visit accordingly. While there is no entry fee to access the tomb, donations are welcome and help support the maintenance of the site. The crypt of San Francesco al Corso is wheelchair accessible, ensuring that all visitors can experience its beauty and tranquility. Photography is permitted within the crypt, allowing travelers to capture memories of their visit. Additionally, guided tours may be available for those who wish to learn more about the history and significance of Juliet's Tomb and the surrounding church.

4.9 Teatro Romano

Teatro Romano, a hidden gem that offers a captivating journey into the city's rich history and cultural heritage. While Verona is renowned for its Shakespearean connections and romantic allure, Teatro Romano stands as a testament to its Roman past, providing visitors with a glimpse into the ancient world. Here, we embark on a detailed exploration of top attractions within Teatro Romano that promise to leave a lasting impression on any traveler.

Teatro Romano Ruins

At the heart of Teatro Romano lies the eponymous Roman theater, a structure that once served as a venue for gladiatorial contests, theatrical performances, and public gatherings. Built in the 1st century BC, this ancient amphitheater boasts an impressive architectural design, with semicircular seating tiers carved into the hillside. Visitors can wander through the well-preserved ruins, imagining the spectacles that once unfolded within its walls. The theater's historical significance, coupled with its picturesque setting overlooking the Adige River, makes it a must-visit attraction in Verona. Entry to the ruins typically requires a nominal fee, which contributes to the preservation of this archaeological treasure.

Archaeological Museum

Adjacent to the Teatro Romano ruins stands the Archaeological Museum, a repository of artifacts that shed light on Verona's Roman past. Housed within a Renaissance-era monastery, the museum showcases a diverse collection of sculptures, mosaics, inscriptions, and everyday objects unearthed from archaeological excavations in Verona and its surroundings. Exhibits provide insight into various aspects of Roman life, including religion, politics, and daily routines. Visitors can marvel at intricate artworks, such as the famous "Head of Serapis," and gain a deeper understanding of Verona's role in the ancient world. The museum's modest entry fee supports ongoing research and preservation efforts.

Lapidary Museum

A hidden gem within Teatro Romano is the Lapidary Museum, which features a remarkable collection of ancient Roman inscriptions and architectural fragments. Located in a 16th-century palace adjacent to the archaeological site, the museum offers a glimpse into the artistic and linguistic heritage of ancient Verona. Visitors can admire intricately carved tombstones, dedicatory plaques, and fragments of monumental buildings, each bearing witness to the city's vibrant past. The museum provides a unique opportunity to explore the evolution of Latin epigraphy and its significance in Roman society. Entry to the Lapidary Museum is often included with admission to the Archaeological Museum, making it a worthwhile addition to any visit to Teatro Romano.

Giardino Archeologico

Surrounding the Teatro Romano ruins is the Giardino Archeologico, an archaeological park that showcases ancient remains and reconstructions amidst lush greenery. This tranquil oasis offers visitors a peaceful retreat from the bustling streets of Verona, allowing them to wander among Roman columns, statues, and architectural fragments. The garden's layout reflects the ancient urban fabric of Verona, providing insight into the city's historical development. Visitors can enjoy leisurely strolls, picnics, or moments of contemplation while surrounded by millennia of history. Entry to the Giardino Archeologico is typically free, making it an accessible and enriching experience for all.

Via Postumia

Adjacent to Teatro Romano runs Via Postumia, an ancient Roman road that once connected the Po River Valley to the Adriatic coast. This historic thoroughfare played a vital role in Verona's development as a major hub of commerce and communication in antiquity. Today, visitors can stroll along Via Postumia, tracing the footsteps of ancient travelers and imagining the sights and sounds of Roman Verona. The street is lined with archaeological remains, including sections of the original pavement and traces of shops and workshops. Walking along Via Postumia offers a tangible connection to Verona's past and provides a unique perspective on the city's urban landscape.

4.10 Borgo Trento District

In Verona lies the Borgo Trento district, a hidden gem waiting to be discovered by intrepid travelers. While often overshadowed by the more famous attractions of the city center, Borgo Trento offers a unique blend of history, culture, and charm that is not to be missed. From picturesque parks to quaint cafes and fascinating museums, this district has something for everyone. Let us delve into top attractions that make Borgo Trento a must-visit destination in Verona.

The Serene Giardino Giusti

One of the crown jewels of Borgo Trento is the Giardino Giusti, a serene oasis that transports visitors to another era. Located on the eastern side of Verona, this meticulously manicured garden is easily accessible from the city center by foot or public transportation. The entry fee, though modest, grants access to a world of beauty and tranquility. Giardino Giusti is steeped in history, dating back to the late 16th century when it was created by the Giusti family. The garden's Renaissance layout, complete with symmetrical designs, ornate fountains, and manicured hedges, is a testament to the family's wealth and taste. Visitors can stroll through the garden, admiring its beauty and taking in the breathtaking views of Verona from the panoramic terrace.

The Charming Piazza Borgo Trento

At the heart of the Borgo Trento district lies Piazza Borgo Trento, a charming square that captures the essence of local life. Surrounded by historic buildings, quaint cafes, and bustling markets, this piazza is a vibrant hub of activity and culture. Located just a short walk from the city center, it is easily accessible by foot or public transportation. Piazza Borgo Trento is more than just a picturesque square; it is a reflection of Verona's rich cultural heritage. Visitors can immerse themselves in the lively atmosphere, savoring the aroma of freshly brewed coffee and the sounds of street musicians. The square is also home to a weekly market, where locals gather to buy fresh produce, artisanal goods, and handmade crafts.

The Fascinating Museo di Castelvecchio

Perched on the banks of the Adige River, overlooking the Borgo Trento district, is the Museo di Castelvecchio, a fascinating museum housed within a medieval fortress. The museum is located just a short walk from Piazza Borgo Trento and is easily accessible by foot or public transportation. Entry fees vary depending on exhibitions, but the experience is well worth the cost. The Museo di Castelvecchio is renowned for its extensive collection of art and artifacts, spanning from the medieval period to the 18th century. Visitors can explore the museum's galleries, which are filled with masterpieces by renowned artists such as Paolo Veronese, Jacopo Bellini, and Andrea Mantegna. The museum also houses a vast collection of medieval weaponry, armor, and archaeological finds, providing insight into Verona's rich history.

The Tranquil Parco delle Mura

For those seeking respite from the urban bustle, the Parco delle Mura offers a tranquil retreat amidst the historic walls of Borgo Trento. Located just a short distance from the Museo di Castelvecchio, this sprawling park is easily accessible and free to enter, making it an ideal destination for a leisurely stroll or a relaxing picnic. The Parco delle Mura is steeped in history, with sections of the ancient city walls still intact. Visitors can wander along the tree-lined pathways, taking in panoramic views of the city and the surrounding countryside. The park is also home to lush greenery, flower gardens, and shaded benches, providing plenty of opportunities for relaxation and contemplation.

The Authentic Trattorias and Cafes

No visit to Borgo Trento would be complete without indulging in the culinary delights of the district's authentic trattorias and cafes. From cozy wine bars to family-run eateries, Borgo Trento offers a wealth of dining options that cater to every palate and budget. Located throughout the district, these establishments are easily accessible and provide a taste of Veronese cuisine at its finest. Trattorias in Borgo Trento serve up traditional dishes made with fresh, locally sourced ingredients, such as risotto, polenta, and hearty meat stews. Visitors can sample regional specialties like pastissada de caval, a slow-cooked horse meat dish, or baccalà alla vicentina, salted cod prepared in a savory sauce. Pair your meal with a glass of Valpolicella wine, produced in the nearby vineyards, for an authentic Veronese dining experience.

4.11 Sports, Outdoor Activities and Adventures

Verona also offers a wealth of outdoor activities and adventures for the intrepid traveler. From cycling along scenic routes to exploring rugged trails in the surrounding hills, Verona provides ample opportunities to immerse oneself in nature and embrace the spirit of adventure. Here, we delve into diverse sports and outdoor activities that promise to ignite the senses and create lasting memories in Verona's stunning surroundings.

Cycling in Valpolicella

Located just a short distance from the city center, Valpolicella beckons cyclists with its rolling hills, vineyard-draped landscapes, and charming villages. This renowned wine-producing region offers a plethora of cycling routes suitable for all skill levels, from leisurely rides through vineyards to challenging ascents amidst breathtaking scenery. Cyclists can explore quaint villages such as San Pietro in Cariano and Fumane, stopping to sample local wines and gastronomic delights along the way. Several tour operators in Verona offer guided cycling tours of Valpolicella, providing participants with expert guidance, rental bikes, and optional wine tastings. Cycling in Valpolicella offers a unique blend of outdoor adventure, cultural immersion, and gastronomic delights, making it a must-do activity for visitors to Verona. Official Website: (https://www.valpolicellaweb.it/en/).

Hiking in Lessinia Regional Park

For those seeking a more rugged outdoor adventure, Lessinia Regional Park offers a pristine wilderness to explore. Located northeast of Verona, this vast natural reserve encompasses lush forests, limestone plateaus, and rugged peaks, providing ample opportunities for hiking, trekking, and wildlife spotting. Trails meander through ancient beech forests, past cascading waterfalls, and up to panoramic viewpoints, offering hikers a chance to immerse themselves in the beauty of the Italian Alps. Guided hiking tours are available for those wishing to explore the park with expert local guides, who provide insights into the region's flora, fauna, and geological formations. Hiking in Lessinia Regional Park promises an unforgettable outdoor adventure amidst unspoiled natural beauty. Official Website:(http://www.parcodellessinia.it/en/).

Rock Climbing in the Adige Valley

Thrill-seekers and outdoor enthusiasts can test their skills on the limestone cliffs of the Adige Valley, just a short drive from Verona. This scenic valley offers a variety of climbing routes suitable for climbers of all abilities, from beginners to seasoned pros. With its unique geological features and stunning vistas, the Adige Valley provides a picturesque backdrop for rock climbing adventures. Several local outfitters and climbing schools offer guided climbing excursions, providing participants with professional instruction, safety equipment, and access to the best climbing spots in the area. Whether scaling vertical walls or bouldering amidst lush riverbanks, rock climbing in the Adige Valley offers an adrenaline-fueled experience in the heart of nature. Official Website:(https://www.verona.net/).

Kayaking on Lake Garda: For water enthusiasts, Lake Garda offers an idyllic setting for kayaking adventures amidst crystal-clear waters and dramatic scenery. Just a short drive from Verona, Italy's largest lake provides a playground for kayakers of all skill levels, with its calm bays, secluded coves, and towering cliffs. Kayakers can paddle along the shoreline, exploring hidden caves, rocky outcrops, and charming lakeside villages. Several tour operators in Verona offer guided kayaking excursions on Lake Garda, providing participants with rental equipment, safety briefings, and knowledgeable guides. Whether gliding past medieval castles or snorkeling in turquoise waters, kayaking on Lake Garda promises an unforgettable aquatic adventure in the heart of northern Italy. Official Website:(https://www.lagodigarda.net/).

Paragliding over Monte Baldo: For the ultimate adrenaline rush and bird's-eye view of Verona's stunning landscapes, paragliding over Monte Baldo is an experience not to be missed. Located on the eastern shore of Lake Garda, Monte Baldo boasts ideal conditions for paragliding, with its gentle thermals, clear skies, and panoramic vistas. Participants can soar like birds, taking in sweeping views of the lake, surrounding mountains, and picturesque villages below. Several paragliding schools and operators in the area offer tandem flights for beginners, allowing participants to experience the thrill of flight under the guidance of experienced pilots. Paragliding over Monte Baldo offers a unique perspective on Verona's natural beauty and is sure to leave adventurers with memories that will last a lifetime. Official Website: (https://www.montebaldo.it/en/).

4.12 Recommended Tour Operators and Guided Tours
Embarking on a journey to explore the enchanting city of Verona is an experience filled with history, culture, and romance. To make the most of your visit, guided tours and expert tour operators can offer invaluable insights, local knowledge, and personalized experiences that enhance your exploration of this

captivating destination. Let's delve into recommended tour operators and guided tours in Verona that promise unforgettable adventures and enriching encounters.

Verona Explorer: Verona Explorer stands out as a premier tour operator offering immersive cultural experiences that showcase the city's rich heritage and hidden gems. Based in the heart of Verona, Verona Explorer provides a range of guided tours led by knowledgeable local guides who are passionate about sharing their love for the city. From walking tours of Verona's historic center to wine tasting excursions in the surrounding countryside, Verona Explorer caters to diverse interests and preferences. Prices for tours vary depending on the duration and activities included, with options available for solo travelers, couples, and groups. For more information and to book your Verona Explorer experience, visit their official website: (https://www.veronaexplorer.com/).

Verona Bike Tour: For those seeking a more active and eco-friendly way to explore Verona, the Verona Bike Tour offers an exciting alternative to traditional guided tours. Located near the city center, Verona Bike Tour provides guided cycling excursions that allow you to discover Verona's landmarks, parks, and scenic pathways from a unique perspective. Prices for Verona Bike Tour vary depending on the duration and route, with options available for leisurely rides through the city streets or more challenging routes that venture into the surrounding countryside. All tours include bike rental, safety equipment, and the expertise of experienced guides who ensure a safe and enjoyable experience for all participants. For more information and to book your Verona Bike Tour, visit their official website: (https://www.veronabiketour.com/).

Verona Food Tour: No visit to Verona would be complete without indulging in its culinary delights and gastronomic treasures. The Verona Food Tour offers a delectable journey through the city's vibrant food scene, led by expert guides who are passionate about local cuisine and culture. Located in the historic center of Verona, the Verona Food Tour offers a variety of tasting experiences that highlight the flavors and traditions of Venetian cuisine. Prices for tours vary depending on the duration and number of tastings included, with options available for foodies of all appetites and preferences. For more information and to book your Verona Food Tour, visit their official website:(https://www.veronafoodtour.com/).

Verona Wine Tour: Immerse yourself in the world of Italian wine with the Verona Wine Tour, a guided exploration of Veneto's renowned vineyards and wineries. Located in the outskirts of Verona, the Verona Wine Tour offers a range of wine tasting experiences that showcase the region's diverse terroir and grape varietals. What makes the Verona Wine Tour exceptional is its access to exclusive wineries and behind-the-scenes experiences that offer a deeper understanding of winemaking traditions and techniques. Whether you prefer crisp whites, full-bodied reds, or sparkling prosecco, the Verona Wine Tour promises a journey of discovery and delight for wine lovers. For more information and to book your Verona Wine Tour, visit their official website: (https://www.veronawinetour.com/).

Verona Walking Tour: Experience the charm and beauty of Verona up close with a guided walking tour that takes you off the beaten path and uncovers hidden gems waiting to be discovered. Based in the historic center of Verona, the Verona Walking Tour offers a range of thematic walks led by local experts who share their insider knowledge and passion for the city. What sets the Verona Walking Tour apart is its emphasis on storytelling and engagement. As you stroll through Verona's cobblestone streets and picturesque piazzas, you'll be captivated by tales of love, intrigue, and historical significance that bring the city's past to life. For more information and to book your Verona Walking Tour, visit their official website: (https://www.veronawalkingtour.com/).

CHAPTER 5
PRACTICAL INFORMATION AND TRAVEL RESOURCES

Scan the QR code with a device to view a comprehensive and larger map of Verona

75

5.1 Maps and Navigation

Navigating Verona is an essential part of your journey. In this guide, we'll delve into the various ways you can access maps and navigate this enchanting city, both offline and digitally.

Verona Tourist Map

For those who prefer the charm of a tangible map, Verona offers a plethora of tourist maps readily available at hotels, information centers, and tourist hotspots. These maps typically highlight key attractions, landmarks, streets, and public transportation routes, providing visitors with a comprehensive overview of the city's layout. You can easily pick up a map upon arrival or request one from your accommodation to aid in your exploration of Verona's treasures.

Accessing Offline Maps

Carrying a paper map ensures you're never without guidance, especially in areas with limited internet connectivity or when your digital device runs out of battery. In Verona, obtaining an offline map is as simple as visiting a local bookstore, souvenir shop, or tourist information center. Many establishments offer pocket-sized maps that fit snugly into your bag or pocket, allowing for convenient reference as you navigate the city's cobblestone streets and winding alleys.

Digital Maps

In today's digital age, accessing maps on your smartphone or tablet has become increasingly popular and convenient. Verona boasts a variety of digital mapping options, ranging from mobile apps to online platforms, designed to enhance your navigation experience. These digital maps often feature interactive functionalities, such as zooming, routing, and location sharing, making them invaluable tools for travelers seeking real-time guidance.

Means of Accessing Verona's Digital Maps

Mobile Apps: Several mobile applications, such as Google Maps, Apple Maps, and Citymapper, offer detailed maps of Verona that can be accessed with just a few taps on your device. These apps provide turn-by-turn directions, public transportation schedules, and points of interest, ensuring seamless navigation throughout the city.

Online Platforms: Numerous websites and online platforms provide digital maps of Verona that can be accessed via any internet-enabled device. Whether you're planning your itinerary from the comfort of your hotel room or seeking directions on the go, these platforms offer comprehensive maps that cater to your needs.

QR Codes: Many guidebooks, brochures, and tourist information materials feature QR codes that link directly to digital maps of Verona. By simply scanning the QR code with your smartphone or tablet, you can instantly access an interactive map that facilitates effortless exploration of the city's attractions and landmarks.

Comprehensive Digital Map

To further streamline your navigation experience, we've included a link and QR code in this guidebook that lead to a comprehensive map of Verona. By clicking on the link or scanning the QR code with your device, you'll gain access to an interactive map equipped with features such as customizable routes, offline mode, and detailed information about each point of interest. This digital map serves as your virtual companion, guiding you through Verona's enchanting streets and helping you uncover hidden gems along the way.

5.2 Five Days Itinerary

Upon arrival in Verona, take some time to settle into your accommodation and freshen up after your journey. Start your exploration of the city by embarking on a leisurely walk through the historic center, soaking in the enchanting atmosphere of Verona's cobblestone streets and medieval architecture. Begin at Piazza Bra, home to the iconic Verona Arena, an ancient Roman amphitheater that serves as the centerpiece of the city's cultural scene. Take a moment to marvel at the arena's grandeur before strolling along Via Mazzini, Verona's main shopping street, lined with charming boutiques and cafes. Continue your walk to Juliet's House (Casa di Giulietta), where you can snap a photo on the famous balcony immortalized in Shakespeare's "Romeo and Juliet."

Day 2: Historical Marvels and Artistic Treasures

Dedicate your second day in Verona to exploring its rich history and artistic heritage. Begin your morning with a visit to Castelvecchio, a majestic medieval castle that houses a remarkable collection of art and artifacts. Wander through the castle's corridors and courtyards, admiring works by renowned artists such as Titian and Veronese. Afterward, make your way to the Duomo di Verona, the city's stunning cathedral adorned with intricate marble carvings and frescoes. Climb the bell tower for panoramic views of Verona's skyline before venturing to the nearby Basilica di San Zeno Maggiore, a masterpiece of Romanesque architecture.

Day 3: Wine Tasting in the Valpolicella Region

Escape the city for a day of indulgence in the picturesque Valpolicella wine region, located just a short drive from Verona. Join a guided tour of local wineries, where you can sample a variety of renowned Valpolicella wines, including Amarone and Valpolicella Ripasso. Learn about the winemaking process from knowledgeable experts as you explore vineyards nestled amidst rolling hills and olive groves. Enjoy a leisurely lunch at a traditional trattoria, savoring regional specialties paired with exquisite wines. Afterward, continue your exploration of the Valpolicella countryside, visiting charming villages and historic estates.

Day 4: Day Trip to Lake Garda

Spend your fourth day in Verona embarking on a day trip to the enchanting Lake Garda, Italy's largest lake. Start your journey with a scenic drive along the shores of Lake Garda, stopping at picturesque towns such as Sirmione, known for its thermal baths and medieval castle. Explore the narrow streets and waterfront promenades, taking in panoramic views of the sparkling lake and surrounding mountains. If you're feeling adventurous, embark on a boat cruise to discover hidden coves and charming islands scattered across the lake. Return to Verona in the evening, refreshed and rejuvenated after a day spent amidst the natural beauty of Lake Garda.

Day 5: Culinary Delights and Farewell to Verona

On your final day in Verona, indulge in the city's culinary delights before bidding farewell to this enchanting destination. Start your day with a traditional Italian breakfast of cappuccino and pastries at a local cafe, savoring the flavors of freshly baked goods and aromatic espresso. Embark on a culinary tour of Verona's gastronomic highlights, sampling regional specialties such as risotto all'Amarone, baccalà alla vicentina, and gelato artigianale. Before departing, take one last stroll through Verona's historic center, savoring the sights and sounds of this timeless city. Reflect on your unforgettable experiences in Verona as you prepare to journey home, carrying memories of its beauty and charm with you forever.

5.3 Essential Packing List

Embarking on a journey to Verona, Italy, requires careful consideration of your packing essentials to ensure a comfortable and enjoyable experience in this enchanting city. From versatile clothing options to practical accessories, here's a comprehensive guide to help you prepare for your visit to Verona.

Clothing for Varied Weather Conditions

Verona experiences a Mediterranean climate characterized by hot summers and cool winters, with moderate temperatures prevailing throughout much of the year. When packing attire for your trip, opt for lightweight, breathable fabrics such as cotton and linen to stay cool during the warmer months. However, it's essential to pack layers, including sweaters or light jackets, as evenings can be cooler, particularly in the shoulder seasons of spring and autumn. If you plan to explore Verona's scenic landscapes or nearby vineyards, comfortable walking shoes are a must, ensuring both style and practicality as you navigate the city's cobblestone streets and countryside paths.

Accessories for Sightseeing and Exploration

To make the most of your explorations in Verona, consider packing a few essential accessories to enhance your sightseeing experiences. A sturdy backpack or crossbody bag is ideal for carrying your camera, water bottle, sunscreen, and other daily essentials as you wander through the city's historic landmarks and vibrant markets. Don't forget to bring a wide-brimmed hat or sunglasses to shield yourself from the sun's rays while strolling along Verona's picturesque streets or visiting outdoor attractions such as the Giardino Giusti or Ponte Pietra.

Practical Items for Comfort and Convenience

In addition to clothing and accessories, packing a few practical items can enhance your comfort and convenience during your stay in Verona. Consider bringing a compact umbrella or lightweight raincoat, especially if you're visiting during the spring or autumn months when brief showers are common. Additionally, a universal travel adapter ensures that you can charge your electronic devices and stay connected throughout your journey. For those planning to indulge in Verona's renowned culinary scene, a reusable water bottle and portable cutlery set can help reduce waste and ensure you stay hydrated and nourished while on the go.

Documents and Essentials for Peace of Mind

Before embarking on your trip to Verona, it's essential to organize your travel documents and essentials to streamline your journey and ensure peace of mind throughout your stay. Be sure to pack your passport, travel insurance information, and any necessary visas or identification documents, keeping them secure in a travel wallet or document organizer. Additionally, carrying copies of important documents, such as your itinerary and emergency contact information, can prove invaluable in the event of unforeseen circumstances. Finally, don't forget to pack any necessary medications, along with a basic first-aid kit, to address any minor health concerns that may arise during your travels.

5.4 Visa Requirements and Entry Procedures

Verona beckons travelers from around the globe with its timeless allure. Before embarking on a journey to this enchanting city, it's imperative to understand the visa requirements and entry procedures, ensuring a smooth and hassle-free experience. Whether arriving by air, train, or road, navigating the entry process sets the stage for an unforgettable exploration of Verona's wonders.

Visa Requirements

For many visitors, the first step in planning a trip to Verona involves understanding the visa requirements. Italy, being a member of the Schengen Area, extends its visa policies to Verona, offering seamless travel for citizens of Schengen member states. Travelers from these countries can enter Verona visa-free for up to 90 days within a 180-day period, provided their passport remains valid for at least three months beyond the intended stay.

Entry Procedures by Air Travel

Arriving in Verona by air unveils a seamless entry process, facilitated by Verona Airport (Valerio Catullo Airport). Upon disembarking, travelers proceed to passport control, where they present their passports and any required documentation, such as visas or entry permits. After clearance, visitors retrieve their luggage and transition to the arrivals area, where they can access various transportation options, including taxis, buses, and rental cars, to reach their desired destination within Verona.

Entry Procedures by Train

For those opting for a scenic journey, arriving in Verona by train offers an enchanting introduction to the city's charms. Verona Porta Nuova railway station serves as a bustling gateway, welcoming travelers from across Italy and beyond. Upon arrival, passengers navigate through the station to reach passport control, where officials verify travel documents before granting entry. Once cleared, visitors emerge onto the bustling streets of Verona, ready to immerse themselves in its rich tapestry of history and culture.

Entry Procedures by Road

Travelers venturing to Verona by road are greeted by well-maintained highways and picturesque landscapes as they approach the city. Upon reaching Verona's outskirts, travelers encounter border checkpoints, where officials conduct routine inspections to ensure compliance with entry requirements. Passport and visa checks may be conducted, particularly for visitors arriving from non-Schengen countries. Once cleared, travelers proceed into Verona, where a world of exploration awaits.

5.5 Safety Tips and Emergency Contacts

Ensuring your safety during your visit to Verona is paramount to enjoying a worry-free experience exploring this enchanting city. From navigating unfamiliar streets to encountering unforeseen circumstances, being prepared and informed is key to safeguarding yourself and your travel companions. In this guide, we'll discuss essential safety tips and provide emergency contacts to assist you in case of need during your time in Verona.

Safety Tips

Awareness of Surroundings: Stay alert and aware of your surroundings, especially in crowded tourist areas and public transportation hubs. Keep an eye on your belongings and be cautious of pickpockets, particularly in busy markets and popular attractions.

Secure Valuables: Keep your valuables, such as passports, money, and electronic devices, secure at all times. Consider using a money belt or hidden pouch to store important items, and avoid carrying large sums of cash or flashy jewelry that may attract unwanted attention.

Stay in Well-Lit Areas: When exploring Verona after dark, stick to well-lit streets and avoid poorly lit or deserted areas. Travel in groups whenever possible and trust your instincts if a situation feels unsafe.

Respect Local Customs: Familiarize yourself with local customs and cultural norms to avoid inadvertently causing offense or misunderstanding. Dress modestly when visiting religious sites and adhere to any posted guidelines or regulations.

Use Licensed Transportation: Opt for licensed taxis and reputable transportation services to ensure your safety while getting around Verona. Avoid accepting rides from unmarked vehicles or individuals who approach you on the street, especially late at night.

83

Hydrate and Sun Protection: Stay hydrated, especially during the warmer months, by carrying a water bottle with you and drinking regularly. Apply sunscreen and wear a hat to protect yourself from the sun's rays, particularly if you'll be spending extended periods outdoors.

Emergency Contacts

In case of an emergency, dial 112, the universal emergency number in Italy, to reach police, ambulance, or fire services. Operators are available 24/7 to assist you in any urgent situation.

Tourist Police (Polizia di Stato - Reparto Prevenzione Crimine): The Tourist Police specialize in assisting visitors to Italy and can provide guidance, support, and assistance in various languages. You can reach the Tourist Police by dialing 113.

Medical Assistance: For medical emergencies or healthcare needs, dial 118 to request an ambulance or seek assistance from medical professionals. Verona boasts several hospitals and medical clinics equipped to handle a range of medical issues.

Consular Assistance: If you're a foreign national in need of consular assistance, contact your country's embassy or consulate in Italy. They can provide support with passport issues, legal matters, and other consular services.

5.6 Currency Exchange and Banking Services

Managing your finances effectively is essential for a smooth and enjoyable visit to Verona. From understanding the local currency to accessing banking services and budgeting for your trip, proper financial planning ensures you can make the most of your time exploring this beautiful city. In this guide, we'll delve into currency exchange, banking options, budgeting tips, and other money matters to help you navigate Verona with confidence.

Currency Exchange

The official currency of Italy, including Verona, is the Euro (EUR). It's advisable to exchange currency before your trip or upon arrival at Verona to ensure you have cash on hand for immediate expenses such as transportation, meals, and souvenirs. While major credit and debit cards are widely accepted in Verona, smaller establishments and markets may prefer cash payments.

Banking Services

Verona offers a variety of banking services to cater to the needs of visitors, including currency exchange, ATM withdrawals, and financial assistance. Here are five banks in Verona and some of their special services for tourists:

UniCredit Bank

UniCredit Bank offers multi-currency accounts and foreign currency exchange services for international travelers.

-Locations: Piazza delle Erbe, 22, 37121 Verona VR; Via Cappello, 4, 37121 Verona VR.

Intesa Sanpaolo

Intesa Sanpaolo provides international money transfer services and foreign currency exchange at competitive rates.

-Locations: Via Leoncino, 12, 37121 Verona VR; Piazza Bra, 25, 37121 Verona VR.

Banca Popolare di Verona

Banca Popolare di Verona offers personalized banking services and assistance in multiple languages for international clients.

-Locations: Piazza delle Erbe, 17, 37121 Verona VR; Corso Porta Nuova, 88, 37122 Verona VR.

Banca Monte dei Paschi di Siena

Banca Monte dei Paschi di Siena provides travel insurance services and assistance with international transactions.

-Locations: Via Diaz, 19, 37121 Verona VR; Piazza Bra, 19, 37121 Verona VR.

Banco BPM

Banco BPM offers prepaid travel cards and currency exchange services tailored to the needs of tourists.

-Locations: Via Giuseppe Garibaldi, 2, 37121 Verona VR; Via Antonio Provolo, 8, 37121 Verona VR.

Budgeting Tips

To make the most of your budget while visiting Verona, consider the following tips:

- *Set a daily spending limit and stick to it to avoid overspending.*
- *Take advantage of free or discounted attractions, such as museums with free admission days or guided walking tours.*
- *Enjoy affordable dining options, such as local trattorias and street food vendors, for delicious meals without breaking the bank.*
- *Use public transportation or walk to explore the city, saving money on transportation costs.*

Bureau de Change

For currency exchange services in Verona, you can visit Bureau de Change establishments located in convenient areas such as: Piazza Bra, Piazza delle Erbe, Via Mazzini

5.7 Language, Communication and Useful Phrases

Verona stands as a testament to history, culture, and romance. As you embark on your journey to this enchanting city, it's essential to equip yourself not only with a sense of wonder but also with some useful linguistic tools to enhance your experience. From navigating the labyrinthine streets to indulging in delectable cuisine, here's a comprehensive guide to language, communication, and essential phrases for your visit to Verona.

Italian Language Essentials

While English is spoken and understood in many tourist areas, having a basic grasp of Italian can enrich your interactions and open doors to authentic experiences. Start with simple greetings like "Ciao" (Hello) and "Buongiorno" (Good morning) to establish a friendly rapport with locals. "Grazie" (Thank you) and "Prego" (You're welcome) are indispensable expressions of gratitude and politeness. If you're seeking assistance, "Scusi" (Excuse me) or "Mi scusi" (Pardon me) can help you politely attract someone's attention.

Navigating Verona

Verona's old town, a UNESCO World Heritage Site, is a labyrinth of narrow cobblestone streets and charming piazzas. While GPS navigation can be helpful, don't hesitate to ask for directions if you find yourself lost. Polite phrases like "Mi può aiutare, per favore?" (Can you help me, please?) coupled with a smile can often lead to friendly guidance from locals. Remember to refer to places by their Italian names, such as "Piazza delle Erbe" instead of "Market Square," to avoid confusion.

Cultural Sensitivities

Embracing local customs and etiquette fosters meaningful connections with the community. When entering shops or restaurants, a friendly "Buongiorno" or "Buonasera" (Good evening) sets a respectful tone. In Verona, it's customary to greet people with a handshake or a kiss on the cheek, depending on your level of familiarity. Additionally, addressing individuals with formal titles like "Signore" (Mr.) and "Signora" (Mrs.) demonstrates courtesy and respect.

Dining Etiquette

Italian cuisine is a cornerstone of Veronese culture, and dining out offers a delightful culinary adventure. When perusing menus, don't hesitate to ask for recommendations with phrases like "Cosa mi consiglia?" (What do you recommend?) or "Qual è il piatto del giorno?" (What is the dish of the day?). Upon receiving your meal, express your appreciation with a sincere "Buon appetito!" (Enjoy your meal!) and conclude the dining experience with a gracious "Grazie, è stato tutto delizioso" (Thank you, it was all delicious).

Engaging in Cultural Activities

Verona's rich cultural heritage extends beyond its architectural marvels to encompass theatrical performances, art exhibitions, and festivals. If you're attending a performance at the iconic Arena di Verona, expressing admiration with phrases like "È spettacolare!" (It's spectacular!) can convey your enthusiasm. For art enthusiasts exploring the city's museums and galleries, expressions like "Questa opera è stupenda" (This artwork is stunning) demonstrate appreciation for the creative masterpieces on display.

Exploring Verona's Surroundings

Verona serves as a gateway to the picturesque countryside of the Veneto region, where rolling vineyards and historic villas await exploration. If you're venturing beyond the city limits, phrases like "Quanto dista da Verona?" (How far is it from Verona?) can help you plan your excursions efficiently. Whether you're embarking on a wine tasting tour in Valpolicella or visiting the romantic shores of Lake Garda, embracing the local language enriches your travel experience and fosters meaningful connections with the community.

5.8 Shopping and Souvenirs

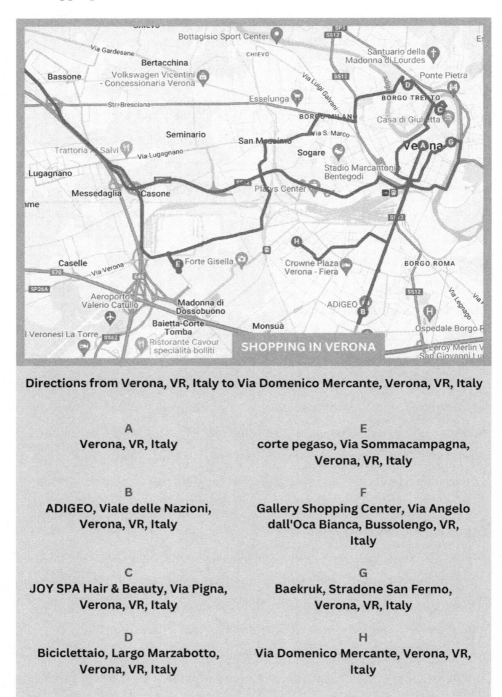

Directions from Verona, VR, Italy to Via Domenico Mercante, Verona, VR, Italy

A
Verona, VR, Italy

B
ADIGEO, Viale delle Nazioni, Verona, VR, Italy

C
JOY SPA Hair & Beauty, Via Pigna, Verona, VR, Italy

D
Biciclettaio, Largo Marzabotto, Verona, VR, Italy

E
corte pegaso, Via Sommacampagna, Verona, VR, Italy

F
Gallery Shopping Center, Via Angelo dall'Oca Bianca, Bussolengo, VR, Italy

G
Baekruk, Stradone San Fermo, Verona, VR, Italy

H
Via Domenico Mercante, Verona, VR, Italy

Verona boasts an array of shopping destinations catering to diverse tastes and preferences. In this guide, we'll explore various shopping options in Verona, highlighting the names, locations, types of goods, prices, opening hours, and how to get there, to help visitors make the most of their shopping excursions in this enchanting city.

Adiego

Located in the historic center of Verona, Adiego is a boutique store renowned for its exquisite collection of Italian-made leather goods. From stylish handbags and wallets to high-quality belts and accessories, Adiego offers an impressive selection of leather products crafted with precision and attention to detail. Prices vary depending on the item's design and craftsmanship, with options to suit every budget. Adiego is open from Monday to Saturday, from 10:00 AM to 7:30 PM. Visitors can easily reach Adiego by walking or using public transportation to the city center.

JOY

Situated in the heart of Verona's shopping district, JOY is a trendy clothing store that caters to fashion-forward individuals seeking the latest styles and trends. From chic dresses and casual wear to stylish accessories and footwear, JOY offers a diverse range of apparel for men and women. Prices at JOY are competitive, with regular sales and promotions available throughout the year. The store is open daily from 9:00 AM to 8:00 PM, making it convenient for visitors to shop at their leisure. JOY is easily accessible by walking or using public transportation to Via Giuseppe Mazzini.

MAG

MAG is a contemporary art gallery and concept store located near Piazza delle Erbe in Verona's historic center. This unique establishment showcases a curated selection of artwork, home décor, and lifestyle products created by local artisans and designers. Visitors can browse through an eclectic mix of paintings, sculptures, ceramics, and handmade crafts, each offering a glimpse into Verona's artistic heritage. Prices at MAG vary depending on the artist and medium, with options available for every budget. The gallery is open daily from 10:00 AM to 7:00 PM, welcoming visitors to explore its diverse collection at their leisure.

Bicicletto Nolo

For cycling enthusiasts and outdoor adventurers, Bicicletto Nolo offers a convenient rental service for bicycles and e-bikes in Verona. Located near the city center, this bike rental shop provides visitors with the opportunity to explore Verona's scenic landscapes and historic landmarks on two wheels. Prices for bike rentals vary depending on the duration and type of bike chosen, with affordable options available for individuals and groups. Bicicletto Nolo is open daily from 9:00 AM to 6:00 PM, allowing visitors to embark on their cycling adventures throughout the day.

Corte Pegaso

This boutique shopping destination showcases a curated selection of artisanal products and gourmet delicacies from the Veneto region. Visitors can peruse through locally-made cheeses, wines, olive oils, and traditional Veronese specialties, perfect for indulging in authentic Italian flavors or purchasing as gifts. Prices at Corte Pegaso vary depending on the product's quality and origin, with options available for every palate and budget. The boutique is open from Tuesday to Sunday, from 10:00 AM to 8:00 PM, providing ample opportunity for visitors to explore its culinary treasures.

Gallery Shopping Center

Situated on the outskirts of Verona, Gallery Shopping Center is a sprawling retail complex offering a diverse array of shops, boutiques, and restaurants under one roof. From international fashion brands and designer labels to electronics and home furnishings, the shopping center caters to a wide range of preferences and budgets. Prices at Gallery Shopping Center vary depending on the store and product category, with regular sales and discounts available throughout the year. The center is open daily from 9:00 AM to 9:00 PM, with ample parking and easy access via public transportation.

Magazzini Firme Outlet

Located just outside Verona, Magazzini Firme Outlet is a popular destination for bargain hunters seeking discounted designer fashion and luxury goods. The outlet features a wide selection of clothing, footwear, accessories, and home décor from renowned brands and high-end designers, all at significantly reduced prices. Visitors can enjoy savings of up to 70% off retail prices on a range of products, making it an ideal spot for scoring designer deals. Magazzini Firme Outlet is open daily from 10:00 AM to 8:00 PM, with shuttle services available from Verona city center for added convenience.

Baekruk

Baekruk is a charming antique store located in Verona's historic center, specializing in vintage furniture, décor, and collectibles from various periods and styles. Visitors can explore an eclectic mix of antique treasures, including retro furnishings, ornate mirrors, vintage posters, and decorative objects, each with its own unique story and character. Prices at Baekruk vary depending on the rarity and condition of the item, with options available for both collectors and casual shoppers. The store is open from Monday to Saturday, from 9:30 AM to 7:00 PM, inviting visitors to step back in time and discover timeless treasures.

Domenico

Domenico is a family-owned boutique store located in Verona's historic center, specializing in handcrafted ceramics, pottery, and artisanal gifts. Visitors can browse through an exquisite collection of ceramic tableware, decorative vases, and kitchen accessories, each meticulously crafted by skilled artisans using traditional techniques. Prices at Domenico vary depending on the size and intricacy of the piece, with options available for every taste and budget. The store is open daily from 10:00 AM to 7:30 PM, welcoming visitors to explore its beautiful collection of handmade treasures.

5.9 Health and Wellness Centers

Verona offers an array of health and wellness centers to rejuvenate the body, mind, and soul. From luxurious spas to holistic retreats, here's an exploration of diverse establishments where visitors can embark on a journey of self-care and relaxation.

Serene Spa Sanctuaries

Verona boasts several luxurious spas that provide an oasis of tranquility amid the bustling cityscape. These sanctuaries offer a range of rejuvenating treatments, from indulgent massages and facials to therapeutic body wraps and hydrotherapy sessions. Visitors can unwind in steam rooms, saunas, and whirlpools, immersing themselves in a world of pampering and serenity. With expert therapists and tranquil ambiance, these spas provide an ideal retreat for those seeking to escape the stresses of daily life and embrace holistic wellness.

Yoga and Meditation Studios

For those in search of inner peace and spiritual renewal, Verona is home to various yoga and meditation studios that offer classes and workshops suitable for practitioners of all levels. From hatha and vinyasa flow to mindfulness and guided meditation, these centers provide a nurturing environment for self-discovery and personal growth. Whether you're a beginner or an experienced yogi, joining a session amidst Verona's picturesque surroundings can enhance your well-being and cultivate a sense of harmony and balance within.

Holistic Healing Centers

Verona's holistic healing centers integrate traditional and alternative therapies to promote holistic wellness and vitality. These establishments offer a range of services, including acupuncture, herbal medicine, energy healing, and Ayurvedic consultations, tailored to address individual needs and restore balance to the body, mind, and spirit. With a focus on natural remedies and holistic approaches to health, these centers empower visitors to embark on a journey of self-healing and transformation, fostering a deeper connection with themselves and the world around them.

Fitness and Wellness Clubs

For those seeking to maintain an active lifestyle while traveling, Verona boasts modern fitness and wellness clubs equipped with state-of-the-art facilities and personalized training programs. Visitors can engage in a variety of fitness classes, from yoga and Pilates to spinning and strength training, under the guidance of experienced instructors. Additionally, these clubs often offer amenities such as swimming pools, sauna facilities, and nutritional counseling, providing a comprehensive approach to health and wellness. Whether you're looking to stay fit on the road or embark on a new fitness journey, Verona's fitness clubs cater to diverse needs and preferences.

Thermal Spas and Wellness Resorts

Verona's proximity to natural thermal springs has given rise to a selection of thermal spas and wellness resorts that harness the healing properties of thermal waters for therapeutic purposes. These resorts offer a range of wellness programs, including thermal baths, mud treatments, and hydrotherapy sessions, designed to promote relaxation, alleviate muscle tension, and improve overall well-being. Set amidst lush gardens and scenic landscapes, these thermal spas provide a serene retreat where visitors can immerse themselves in the healing powers of nature and emerge feeling rejuvenated and revitalized.

5.10 Useful Websites, Mobile Apps and Online Resources

The Verona Official Tourism Website serves as a comprehensive guide for visitors, offering a wealth of information on attractions, events, accommodations, dining options, and transportation within the city. Here, travelers can access detailed maps, itineraries, and insider tips to plan their visit effectively. The website also provides updates on current events and festivals happening in Verona, allowing visitors to immerse themselves in the city's vibrant cultural scene. Additionally, the website offers practical information on visa requirements, entry procedures, and safety tips for travelers, ensuring a smooth and enjoyable experience in Verona.

Google Maps

Google Maps is an indispensable tool for navigating Verona's streets and attractions with ease. Whether exploring on foot, by public transport, or by car, travelers can rely on Google Maps to find directions, estimate travel times, and locate points of interest. The app offers detailed maps of Verona's neighborhoods, complete with user reviews and ratings for restaurants, hotels, and attractions. With real-time traffic updates and alternative route suggestions, Google Maps helps visitors navigate the city efficiently, allowing them to make the most of their time in Verona.

Rick Steves' Audio Europe™

For visitors seeking a deeper understanding of Verona's history and culture, Rick Steves' Audio Europe™ app offers a treasure trove of audio guides and walking tours. With expert commentary from travel guru Rick Steves, users can explore Verona's landmarks and hidden gems at their own pace, learning fascinating insights along the way. The app features audio tours of iconic sites such as the Verona Arena, Juliet's House, and Castelvecchio, providing an immersive and educational experience for visitors. Whether wandering through historic piazzas or meandering along ancient cobblestone streets, Rick Steves' Audio Europe™

app enriches the visitor's journey with engaging storytelling and insider knowledge.

Eatwith

For culinary enthusiasts eager to sample authentic Italian cuisine, Eatwith offers a unique dining experience by connecting travelers with local hosts for home-cooked meals and cooking classes. In Verona, visitors can browse a diverse selection of dining experiences, ranging from intimate dinners in private homes to hands-on pasta-making workshops led by passionate cooks. Eatwith provides an opportunity to connect with locals, share stories, and savor homemade dishes prepared with love and care. Whether dining al fresco in a scenic garden or gathering around a family table, Eatwith offers a memorable culinary experience that celebrates the flavors of Verona.

Verona Card Mobile App

The Verona Card Mobile App is a convenient companion for visitors looking to maximize their exploration of the city's attractions while enjoying cost savings. Available for download on smartphones, the app provides access to exclusive discounts, skip-the-line privileges, and special offers at participating museums, galleries, and historic sites in Verona. With the Verona Card Mobile App, visitors can effortlessly plan their itinerary, track their savings, and navigate to featured attractions using interactive maps and directions. Whether exploring the Verona Arena, Juliet's House, or the Archaeological Museum, the Verona Card Mobile App simplifies the visitor experience, making it easier to discover the treasures of Verona while enjoying great value.

5.11 Internet Access and Connectivity

Verona offers a variety of options to access the internet and stay connected during your visit. From reliable Wi-Fi hotspots to mobile data plans, here's a comprehensive overview of five useful internet access and connectivity options for visitors to Verona.

Hotel Wi-Fi Services

Many hotels and accommodations in Verona provide complimentary Wi-Fi access to their guests. Upon check-in, inquire about the availability and quality of Wi-Fi services offered by your hotel. Most establishments offer password-protected Wi-Fi networks, which you can access in your room or common areas such as the lobby or lounge. While hotel Wi-Fi is generally reliable for basic browsing and communication needs, it's important to note that connection speeds may vary depending on the hotel's location and infrastructure.

Public Wi-Fi Hotspots

Verona boasts numerous public Wi-Fi hotspots scattered throughout the city, allowing visitors to stay connected while exploring its charming streets and landmarks. These hotspots are typically located in popular tourist areas, parks, and public squares, providing convenient access to the internet at no cost. Keep in mind that public Wi-Fi networks may have security risks, so exercise caution when accessing sensitive information such as online banking or personal accounts. Additionally, be mindful of data usage limits and connection speeds, which may fluctuate depending on network congestion and demand.

SIM Cards and Mobile Data Plans

For travelers who require continuous internet access during their stay in Verona, purchasing a local SIM card and mobile data plan is a convenient option. Several mobile network providers offer prepaid SIM cards with varying data allowances and validity periods, allowing you to choose a plan that suits your needs and budget. You can purchase SIM cards from official stores, kiosks, or authorized retailers located throughout the city. Once activated, simply insert the

SIM card into your unlocked smartphone or mobile device to access high-speed internet on the go.

Portable Wi-Fi Devices

Another convenient option for internet access in Verona is renting or purchasing a portable Wi-Fi device, also known as a pocket Wi-Fi or mobile hotspot. These compact devices allow you to create a personal Wi-Fi network wherever you go, providing reliable internet connectivity for multiple devices simultaneously. Rental services are available at airports, train stations, and tourist information centers, offering flexible rental periods and competitive pricing options. With a portable Wi-Fi device, you can enjoy seamless internet access without relying on public networks or mobile data plans.

Internet Cafés and Co-Working Spaces

For visitors in need of dedicated workspace or extended internet access, Verona's internet cafés and co-working spaces offer comfortable environments equipped with high-speed internet, workstations, and amenities such as printing and scanning facilities. These establishments cater to digital nomads, remote workers, and travelers seeking a productive environment to stay connected and get work done while away from home. Whether you need to catch up on emails, conduct online research, or attend virtual meetings, internet cafés and co-working spaces provide a convenient solution for your connectivity needs in Verona.

5.12 Visitor Centers and Tourist Assistance

In Verona, you'll find a range of visitor centers and tourist assistance services ready to help make your stay as smooth and enjoyable as possible. From providing maps and information about attractions to offering guidance on transportation and accommodations, these centers are valuable resources for visitors exploring Verona. In this guide, we'll explore the various visitor centers and tourist assistance options available in the city, along with their special services to enhance your experience.

Visitor Centers

Verona Tourist Information Center

Located in the heart of Verona, Piazza Bra, 28, 37121, the Tourist Information Center offers a wealth of information about the city's attractions, events, and services. Visitors can obtain maps, brochures, and guides in multiple languages, as well as receive assistance from knowledgeable staff members. The center also provides booking services for tours, tickets, and accommodations to help you plan your visit efficiently.

Verona Tourist Office at Porta Nuova Railway Station

Conveniently situated at the Porta Nuova Railway Station Piazzale XXV Aprile, 5, 37138, this tourist office caters to travelers arriving in Verona by train. In addition to providing tourist information and assistance, the office offers luggage storage services for travelers who wish to explore the city unencumbered by their bags. Visitors can also purchase Verona Card, which provides access to major attractions and discounts on transportation.

Verona Tourist Office at Verona Airport: For visitors arriving by air, the Verona Tourist Office at Aeroporto Valerio Catullo, 37060 Caselle di Sommacampagna VR is the first point of contact for information and assistance. Staff members are available to answer queries, provide maps, and offer guidance on transportation options from the airport to the city center. Additionally, visitors can purchase Verona Card and arrange airport transfers or transportation services.

Verona Visitor Center at Castelvecchio: Situated near the iconic Castelvecchio 2, 37121 , this visitor center offers a unique setting for obtaining tourist information and assistance. In addition to providing guidance on nearby attractions and points of interest, the center hosts exhibitions, cultural events, and educational programs to enrich visitors' experience of Verona's history and heritage.

Verona Tourism Information Point at Piazza delle Erbe: Located in the bustling Piazza delle Erbe 37121, this information point offers quick access to tourist services and assistance for visitors exploring the historic center of Verona. Staff members can provide recommendations for dining, shopping, and sightseeing, as well as help with booking guided tours and activities in the area.

Special Services of Tourist Assistants

-***Multilingual Staff:*** Many tourist assistance centers in Verona have staff members who speak multiple languages, ensuring effective communication and assistance for international visitors.

-***Guided Tours:*** Some centers offer guided tours led by knowledgeable local guides, providing insights into Verona's history, culture, and landmarks.

-***Verona Card:*** Several visitor centers sell Verona Card, a convenient pass that grants access to major attractions and discounts on transportation, dining, and shopping.

-***Ticket Booking Services:*** Tourist assistants can help visitors book tickets for attractions, events, and transportation services, saving time and hassle during their stay in Verona.

-***Informational Materials:*** Visitors can obtain maps, brochures, and guides from tourist assistance centers, allowing them to navigate Verona and plan their itinerary with ease.

CHAPTER 6
CULINARY DELIGHTS

6.1 Traditional Veronese Cuisine: Risotto and Pastissada de Caval

Veronese cuisine offers a delectable journey through time. The city's dishes, from savory risottos to hearty stews, reflect the essence of Verona's culture and its agrarian past. Visitors to this romantic city are encouraged to explore beyond the architectural marvels and immerse themselves in the flavors that have been perfected over centuries.

Risotto all'Amarone

One cannot speak of Veronese cuisine without extolling the virtues of Risotto all'Amarone, a dish that epitomizes the region's love affair with rice and wine. This creamy risotto is elevated by the addition of Amarone wine, a robust red that imparts a deep, velvety richness to the dish. Prepared with Carnaroli or Vialone Nano rice, the risotto is cooked to perfection, absorbing the flavors of onions, broth, and the star ingredient, Amarone. Visitors can savor this exquisite

101

dish in numerous osterie and ristoranti scattered throughout Verona. Establishments like Osteria del Bugiardo and Antica Bottega del Vino are renowned for their risottos, offering a cozy ambiance that complements the culinary experience. Prices for Risotto all'Amarone typically range from 18 to 25 euros, reflecting the quality of the ingredients and the skill required to prepare this dish. For the best experience, pairing the risotto with a glass of Amarone wine is highly recommended, as it enhances the dish's flavors and provides a harmonious dining experience.

Pastissada de Caval

Pastissada de Caval, a traditional Veronese stew, dates back to the Roman era when horse meat was a staple during times of war and famine. Today, this dish is a beloved delicacy, prepared with marinated horse meat that is slow-cooked with red wine, onions, carrots, and a medley of spices. The result is a rich, flavorful stew that embodies the rustic charm of Verona's culinary heritage. While the idea of eating horse meat may seem unusual to some visitors, those willing to try Pastissada de Caval will find it available in traditional restaurants like Trattoria alla Pergola and Osteria Sottoriva. These establishments honor the authenticity of the dish, ensuring that every bite is a testament to centuries-old recipes. Prices usually range from 15 to 22 euros per serving. It is best enjoyed with a side of polenta, another staple of Veronese cuisine, which perfectly soaks up the stew's savory sauce.

Bollito con la Pearà

Bollito con la Pearà, often considered the ultimate comfort food in Verona, consists of boiled meats served with a distinctive sauce known as pearà. The sauce, made from bread crumbs, beef marrow, broth, and a generous amount of black pepper, has a creamy texture and a peppery kick that complements the tender meats. This dish is traditionally served during festive occasions and family gatherings, symbolizing warmth and togetherness. To experience Bollito con la Pearà, visitors should head to family-run trattorias like Trattoria Al Bersagliere or Ristorante 12 Apostoli, where the dish is prepared with a touch of homely love. The cost of this hearty meal ranges from 20 to 30 euros, often including a selection of meats such as beef, chicken, and pork. Pairing it with a robust local red wine like Valpolicella enhances the dish's flavors and provides a well-rounded culinary experience.

Gnocchi di Patate

Gnocchi di Patate, or potato gnocchi, are soft, pillowy dumplings that hold a special place in Veronese hearts. These delicate morsels are typically served with a variety of sauces, from simple butter and sage to rich tomato-based or meat sauces. The preparation of gnocchi is an art form, requiring just the right balance of potatoes, flour, and a gentle touch to achieve the perfect texture. Verona's trattorias and restaurants, such as Locanda 4 Cuochi and Osteria da Ugo, offer gnocchi dishes that highlight the versatility of this beloved food. Prices for a serving of gnocchi range from 12 to 18 euros, depending on the sauce and accompaniments. For a truly authentic experience, visitors should try Gnocchi di Patate during the annual Carnevale di Verona, when the city celebrates with parades and feasts featuring this classic dish.

Tiramisu

No culinary journey through Verona would be complete without indulging in Tiramisu, the quintessential Italian dessert. Though its origins are debated, Tiramisu holds a special place in Veneto's dessert repertoire. Made with layers of coffee-soaked ladyfingers, mascarpone cheese, eggs, sugar, and cocoa, this dessert is the perfect blend of sweetness and bitterness. Visitors can find exceptional Tiramisu in cafes and pastry shops such as Pasticceria Flego and Pasticceria Cordioli. Prices for a slice of Tiramisu typically range from 5 to 8 euros. For an unforgettable treat, enjoying Tiramisu with a cup of freshly brewed espresso or a glass of sweet wine like Recioto di Soave is highly recommended.

6.2 Trattorias and Osterias

This enchanting city in the Veneto region of Italy offers a myriad of dining experiences, particularly through its trattorias and osterias. These establishments provide a taste of authentic Veronese cuisine, blending time-honored recipes with the vibrant flavors of the region. For travelers eager to delve into Verona's gastronomic delights, here are notable trattorias and osterias that epitomize the city's culinary heritage.

Trattoria Al Pompiere

Trattoria Al Pompiere is a culinary gem that has been delighting diners for decades. Located near the iconic Piazza delle Erbe, this trattoria is renowned for its traditional Veronese dishes, crafted with love and precision. The ambiance is cozy, adorned with vintage fireman memorabilia, paying homage to its name "The Fireman." The menu at Al Pompiere features a variety of classic dishes, such as "Risotto all'Amarone," a rich and flavorful risotto made with the famous Amarone wine, and "Pastissada de Caval," a slow-cooked horse meat stew, which is a local specialty. Prices are moderate, with main courses ranging from €15 to €25. A helpful tip for visitors is to pair their meal with a glass of local Valpolicella wine, enhancing the dining experience with the region's robust flavors.

Osteria Sottoriva

Osteria Sottoriva, situated along the picturesque Adige River, offers diners a rustic and intimate setting that perfectly complements its hearty menu. This osteria is beloved by both locals and tourists for its genuine atmosphere and delicious food. The outdoor seating area, with its charming view of the river, is especially popular during the warmer months. The menu at Sottoriva is a celebration of regional produce and traditional cooking methods. Signature dishes include "Bigoli con le Sarde," a thick spaghetti-like pasta served with a savory sardine sauce, and "Gnocchi di Patate," soft potato dumplings often accompanied by a rich meat ragù. Prices here are quite reasonable, with most dishes priced between €10 and €20. Visitors should note that the osteria does not take reservations, so arriving early is recommended to secure a table.

Trattoria La Torre

Housed in a historic building near the ancient Torre dei Lamberti, Trattoria La Torre offers a dining experience steeped in history. The interior is elegantly rustic, featuring wooden beams and classic Italian decor, which sets the tone for a memorable meal. The cuisine at La Torre focuses on traditional Veronese and Veneto dishes, prepared with a modern twist. Guests can enjoy specialties such as "Tortellini di Valeggio," delicate tortellini filled with a mixture of meats and herbs, and "Baccalà alla Vicentina," a creamy salt cod dish that is a staple of the region. Main course prices range from €20 to €30, reflecting the high quality of ingredients and the skillful preparation. A useful tip for visitors is to inquire about the daily specials, which often showcase seasonal ingredients and provide a unique taste of Verona.

Osteria del Bugiardo

For those seeking a chic yet authentic dining experience, Osteria del Bugiardo is an excellent choice. Located on the bustling Corso Porta Borsari, this osteria is part of the renowned Buglioni winery, ensuring an exceptional selection of wines to accompany the meal. The menu features a blend of traditional and contemporary dishes, highlighting the best of Veronese cuisine. Popular choices include "Polenta e Soppressa," a dish of creamy polenta served with local cured sausage, and "Tagliata di Manzo," a perfectly cooked sliced beef steak. Prices are mid-range, with dishes typically costing between €15 and €25. Visitors are encouraged to sample the osteria's wine offerings, particularly the Buglioni Amarone, which pairs beautifully with the robust flavors of the food.

Trattoria alla Colonna

Trattoria alla Colonna, located near the historic Porta Borsari, is a beloved establishment known for its warm hospitality and delicious food. This trattoria is a favorite among locals, offering a menu that is both comforting and authentic. Diners can indulge in classic dishes such as "Risotto al Tastasal," a flavorful risotto made with seasoned pork, and "Pasta e Fagioli," a hearty pasta and bean soup that epitomizes rustic Italian cooking. Prices are very reasonable, with most main courses priced between €10 and €20. A tip for visitors is to save room for dessert, as the "Tiramisu" here is often praised as one of the best in Verona.

6.3 Wine Tasting Tours in Valpolicella

Valpolicella is a haven for wine enthusiasts. This picturesque area, known for its exquisite vineyards and timeless winemaking traditions, offers an immersive experience into the world of Italian wines. The essence of Valpolicella can be truly appreciated through its wine tasting tours, which provide not just a sensory delight but also a journey into the rich cultural heritage of the region. Whether you are a seasoned oenophile or a curious beginner, Valpolicella's wine tours are bound to captivate your senses and expand your palate. Here, we explore distinguished wine tasting tours that promise an unforgettable experience.

The Elegance of Amarone at Tenuta Sant'Antonio

Tenuta Sant'Antonio stands as a beacon of excellence in Valpolicella, offering a profound insight into the making of Amarone, one of the region's most renowned wines. Located in the heart of Valpolicella, this estate combines modern viticulture techniques with time-honored traditions. Visitors can indulge in a comprehensive tour that includes a walk through the vineyards, a visit to the aging cellars, and an elaborate tasting session. The tours at Tenuta Sant'Antonio are available through their official website and can be booked in advance. Prices range from €25 to €50 per person, depending on the tour package and the wines included. For a deeper understanding, visitors are advised to opt for the premium tour, which features a tasting of the estate's top-tier wines, paired with local cheeses and cured meats. An important tip for visitors is to wear comfortable shoes, as the tour involves a fair amount of walking through the vineyards.

The Historic Charm of Masi Wine Estate

Masi Wine Estate offers a unique blend of history and innovation, set against the backdrop of the scenic Valpolicella hills. This estate is famed for its production of Amarone and other prestigious wines. The tour at Masi includes a visit to the historic cellars, a walk through the vineyards, and a detailed explanation of the winemaking process, followed by a guided tasting of their signature wines. Tours are available for booking via the Masi Wine Estate's official website, with prices typically starting at €30 per person. For those seeking a more personalized experience, private tours can be arranged at a higher cost. A key tip for visitors is to plan their visit during the spring or fall when the vineyards are at their most beautiful, and the weather is ideal for exploring the estate.

A Modern Twist at Tommasi Viticoltori

Tommasi Viticoltori is a name synonymous with quality and innovation in Valpolicella. This family-owned winery, established in 1902, offers a tour that perfectly balances tradition and modernity. Visitors are treated to a behind-the-scenes look at the winery's state-of-the-art production facilities, as well as the historic cellars where their wines are aged to perfection. Tours at Tommasi can be booked online through their official website, with prices ranging from €20 to €45 per person. The higher-end tours include a tasting of their premium wines, paired with local delicacies. An essential tip for visitors is to take advantage of the knowledgeable guides, who can provide a wealth of information about the wines and the winemaking process, enhancing the overall experience.

The Boutique Experience at Brunelli Wine Estate

For those looking for a more intimate and personalized wine tasting experience, Brunelli Wine Estate is an excellent choice. This boutique winery offers a charming and cozy setting, perfect for a leisurely exploration of Valpolicella's wines. The tour includes a visit to the vineyards, the production area, and the cellars, followed by a relaxed tasting session. Bookings for Brunelli Wine Estate tours can be made through their official website, with prices starting at €25 per person. For a truly memorable experience, visitors can opt for the gourmet tour, which includes a selection of the estate's finest wines paired with artisanal cheeses and charcuterie. A useful tip for visitors is to engage with the winemakers, who are often available during the tours and can share fascinating insights and stories about their wines.

The Organic Delight at Novaia Winery

Novaia Winery stands out for its commitment to organic and sustainable viticulture. This family-run estate, situated in the Valpolicella Classica area, offers a tour that emphasizes their eco-friendly practices and the unique characteristics of their organic wines. Visitors can explore the lush vineyards, learn about organic farming techniques, and enjoy a tasting of Novaia's distinctive wines. Tours can be booked directly through the Novaia Winery's website, with prices typically around €20 to €40 per person. The more comprehensive tours include a tasting of their premium organic wines, paired with local organic produce. A helpful tip for visitors is to inquire about the seasonal variations in their wines, as Novaia's offerings can differ based on the time of year, providing a unique tasting experience with each visit.

6.4 Gelaterias and Dessert Shops

Verona offers a delightful array of gelaterias and dessert shops beckons visitors with promises of sweet indulgence. From artisanal gelato to decadent pastries, Verona's dessert scene offers a tantalizing journey through Italy's culinary traditions.

Gelateria La Romana

Gelateria La Romana stands as a beacon of excellence in Verona's gelato scene, revered for its commitment to crafting artisanal gelato using only the finest ingredients. Located near the bustling Piazza Bra, this gelateria entices passersby with its vibrant displays of creamy confections. Visitors can expect a wide variety of flavors, from classic favorites like Stracciatella to innovative creations such as Pistachio with Sicilian Almonds. Prices at Gelateria La Romana typically range from 2.50 to 4 euros for a small cone or cup, with additional charges for premium flavors or toppings. For the best experience, visitors should arrive early in the day to avoid long lines, especially during peak tourist seasons. Additionally, opting for the signature "crema" topping, a dollop of freshly whipped cream, adds an extra touch of indulgence to the gelato experience.

Pasticceria Perbellini

Pasticceria Perbellini beckons pastry enthusiasts with its tantalizing array of cakes, pastries, and chocolates. Established in 1888, this venerable institution has upheld its legacy of excellence, delighting generations with its artisanal creations. From delicate fruit tarts to rich chocolate truffles, every offering at Pasticceria Perbellini is a work of culinary art. Visitors can indulge in an assortment of treats at Pasticceria Perbellini, with prices varying depending on the selection. A slice of cake typically costs between 4 and 6 euros, while a box of assorted chocolates may range from 10 to 20 euros. For a truly unforgettable experience, patrons can enjoy their sweets in the elegant tearoom, savoring each bite amidst the timeless charm of the historic surroundings.

Gelateria Ponte Pietra

Situated along the picturesque banks of the Adige River, Gelateria Ponte Pietra offers not only delectable gelato but also breathtaking views of Verona's iconic Ponte Pietra bridge. This charming gelateria prides itself on using locally sourced ingredients to create gelato flavors that reflect the essence of the Veneto region. From refreshing fruit sorbets to creamy gelato made with organic milk, Gelateria Ponte Pietra caters to every palate. Prices at Gelateria Ponte Pietra are comparable to other gelaterias in the city, with a small cone or cup typically costing between 2.50 and 4 euros. Visitors can enhance their gelato experience by taking a leisurely stroll along the riverbank, soaking in the beauty of Verona's skyline as they savor each spoonful of creamy goodness. Additionally, the gelateria offers gluten-free and vegan options, ensuring that everyone can indulge in their sweet creations.

Pasticceria Flego

For over a century, Pasticceria Flego has been a beloved destination for those seeking the finest pastries and desserts in Verona. Located near the bustling Piazza delle Erbe, this historic pastry shop delights visitors with its exquisite cakes, cookies, and specialty sweets. Whether craving a classic tiramisu or a delicate mille-feuille, patrons are sure to find a tempting treat at Pasticceria Flego. Prices at Pasticceria Flego vary depending on the selection, with individual pastries typically ranging from 2 to 5 euros. Visitors can also opt to indulge in a traditional Italian breakfast, complete with freshly baked croissants and aromatic espresso. For those looking to take a piece of Verona home with them, the pastry shop offers beautifully packaged gift boxes, perfect for sharing the city's sweet treasures with loved ones.

Gelateria Passaggio

Tucked away in a quaint alleyway near the bustling Via Mazzini, Gelateria Passaggio beckons discerning gelato enthusiasts with its handcrafted flavors and welcoming ambiance. This hidden gem prides itself on using seasonal fruits and locally sourced ingredients to create gelato that captures the essence of Verona's culinary heritage. From creamy hazelnut to zesty lemon sorbet, Gelateria Passaggio offers a delightful array of flavors to tantalize the taste buds. Prices at Gelateria Passaggio are relatively affordable, with a small cone or cup typically costing between 2 and 3.50 euros. Visitors can enjoy their gelato while exploring the charming streets of Verona's historic center, discovering hidden gems and architectural wonders around every corner. Additionally, the gelateria's friendly staff are always eager to offer recommendations and share their passion for gelato, ensuring that every visit is a memorable experience.

Savoring Verona's Sweet Treasures

Verona's gelaterias and dessert shops offer more than just delicious treats—they provide a glimpse into the city's rich culinary heritage and vibrant culture. Whether indulging in artisanal gelato or savoring decadent pastries, visitors are sure to be enchanted by the flavors and aromas that abound in this charming Italian city. With each bite, they embark on a sweet journey through Verona's past and present, creating memories that will linger long after they depart.

6.5 Coffee Culture: Caffè Espresso and Aperitivo Hour

Verona boasts intense shots of espresso to the leisurely Aperitivo hour, Veronese coffee culture is a tapestry of flavors, aromas, and social rituals that provide a unique window into the city's soul. For those eager to explore this aspect of Veronese life, here are five key elements that define Verona's coffee culture, along with notable places to experience them.

Caffè Espresso

In Verona, as throughout Italy, the caffè espresso is more than just a drink; it's a daily ritual, a moment of pause, and a jolt of pure Italian energy. The city's coffee bars are bustling with locals who stop by for a quick espresso shot, often consumed standing at the counter. This tradition is rooted in efficiency and sociability, as the caffè espresso provides a brief yet powerful pause in the day. One of the best places to experience this quintessential Italian coffee is Caffè Borsari, located on Corso Porta Borsari. This historic café offers a superb espresso, rich and aromatic, for about €1.20. Visitors should note that while standing at the bar is the norm and less expensive, sitting down may incur additional charges. For those new to the espresso culture, a friendly tip is to order "un caffè" to seamlessly blend in with the locals.

Cappuccino

While espresso is the go-to throughout the day, cappuccino reigns supreme in the morning hours. A creamy blend of espresso, steamed milk, and a frothy top, cappuccino is typically enjoyed with a pastry for breakfast. Verona's coffee bars open early, catering to the morning crowd that relishes this comforting start to their day. Caffè Wallner, situated near Piazza Bra, is a delightful spot to savor a morning cappuccino. The café's cozy ambiance and selection of freshly baked pastries make it a popular choice. A cappuccino here costs around €1.50 to €2, and pairing it with a "cornetto" (Italian croissant) is highly recommended. It's important to remember that cappuccino is traditionally a morning beverage in Italy, often avoided by locals after 11 AM.

Aperitivo Hour

Aperitivo hour in Verona is an institution, a time when friends and colleagues gather to unwind and socialize over drinks and snacks. While aperitivo often involves cocktails and wine, coffee also plays a central role. Espresso martinis and other coffee-based cocktails are popular choices during this relaxed pre-dinner ritual. La Tradision, located near Piazza delle Erbe, is a vibrant spot to experience aperitivo. This trendy bar offers an extensive menu of coffee cocktails, including their signature espresso martini. Prices for aperitivo drinks range from €5 to €8, typically accompanied by complimentary snacks like olives, bruschetta, and cheeses. A tip for visitors is to arrive early, as aperitivo hour, usually from 6 PM to 8 PM, can get quite busy, especially on weekends.

Caffè Macchiato

For those who find espresso too strong yet cappuccino too milky, the caffè macchiato offers a perfect middle ground. This "stained" coffee, consisting of an espresso with a small amount of steamed milk, provides a balanced flavor that highlights the best of both worlds. It's a versatile choice, enjoyed at any time of the day. Caffè Tubino, near Castelvecchio, serves an excellent macchiato. The café's modern yet welcoming atmosphere makes it a great place to relax and enjoy this balanced coffee. A macchiato here is reasonably priced at about €1.50. Visitors should take the time to appreciate the artistry of Italian baristas, who skillfully prepare each cup with precision and care.

Caffè Corretto

For a more adventurous coffee experience, the caffè corretto offers a spirited twist. This "corrected" coffee typically involves adding a splash of grappa, sambuca, or another liqueur to an espresso, creating a warming and invigorating drink that is particularly popular in the colder months. Antica Bottega del Vino, one of Verona's oldest and most renowned wine bars, also excels in crafting a perfect caffè corretto. Located near Piazza delle Erbe, this historic venue offers a cozy and authentic setting to enjoy this unique beverage. A caffè corretto costs around €3, depending on the chosen liqueur. Visitors are advised to enjoy this drink slowly, savoring the harmonious blend of coffee and spirits.

6.6 Best Fine Dining Restaurants

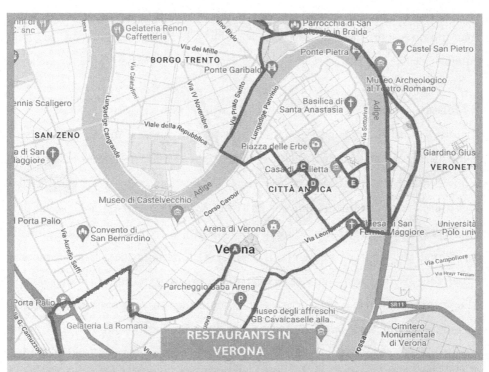

Directions from Verona, VR, Italy to Hotel Villa del Quar, Via Quar, Quar, VR, Italy

A
Verona, VR, Italy

B
Ristorante Oseleta, Località Cordevigo, Cavaion Veronese, VR, Italy

C
Casa Perbellini - 12 Apostoli, Vicolo Corticella San Marco, Verona, VR, Italy

D
Antica Bottega del Vino, Vicolo Scudo di Francia, Verona, VR, Italy

E
Ristorante Il Desco, Via Dietro San Sebastiano, Verona, VR, Italy

F
Hotel Villa del Quar, Via Quar, Quar, VR, Italy

Verona offers a plethora of fine dining restaurants that promise to tantalize the taste buds and provide a feast for the senses. In this guide, we explore the best fine dining establishments in Verona, each offering a unique and exquisite culinary journey.

Ristorante Oseleta

Ristorante Oseleta, nestled in the beautiful surroundings of the Villa Cordevigo Wine Relais, is a sanctuary for gourmands. This Michelin-starred restaurant is renowned for its sophisticated ambiance and meticulously crafted dishes that highlight the finest local ingredients. Chef Giuseppe D'Aquino's menu is a testament to the richness of Italian cuisine, with a modern twist that elevates traditional flavors to new heights. Dining at Ristorante Oseleta is an immersive experience, with a seven-course tasting menu priced at around €130 per person. The restaurant's wine list is extensive, featuring an impressive selection of regional and international wines that perfectly complement the dishes. A tip for visitors is to arrive early to enjoy a leisurely aperitif in the enchanting garden, enhancing the overall dining experience.

Casa Perbellini

Casa Perbellini, located in the heart of Verona, is a culinary gem that showcases the innovative spirit of Chef Giancarlo Perbellini. This intimate, Michelin-starred restaurant offers a dining experience that feels both exclusive and welcoming. The open kitchen concept allows diners to witness the artistry and precision that goes into each dish, creating a dynamic and engaging atmosphere. The menu at Casa Perbellini is a celebration of creativity and seasonality, with prices for the tasting menu starting at approximately €150 per person. The dishes are not only visually stunning but also a harmonious blend of textures and flavors. A useful tip for visitors is to make reservations well in advance, as the limited seating ensures a high demand. The personalized service and attention to detail make every meal here a special occasion.

Antica Bottega del Vino

Antica Bottega del Vino is a historic establishment that has been serving exquisite cuisine since the 16th century. This iconic restaurant and wine bar in Verona's old town is beloved for its authentic atmosphere and extensive wine cellar, which boasts over 4,000 labels. The culinary offerings at Antica Bottega del Vino are a delightful homage to traditional Veronese cuisine, prepared with a refined touch. Diners can expect to spend around €80 to €120 per person for a multi-course meal paired with exceptional wines. The knowledgeable sommeliers are adept at recommending the perfect wine to enhance each dish. For visitors, a valuable tip is to explore the wine cellar, a fascinating treasure trove for oenophiles. The warm, rustic interiors and the rich history of the venue add to the charm and allure of the dining experience.

Il Desco

Il Desco, a Michelin-starred restaurant located in a beautifully restored 14th-century building, offers a sublime dining experience that merges art and gastronomy. Chef Matteo Rizzo's creations are a testament to his culinary expertise and artistic vision, with each dish meticulously designed to delight both the palate and the eyes. The elegant decor and serene ambiance make Il Desco a perfect choice for a luxurious dining experience. The tasting menus at Il Desco range from €120 to €160 per person, featuring innovative dishes that highlight seasonal ingredients and contemporary techniques. A noteworthy tip for visitors is to indulge in the wine pairing option, which enhances the dining experience with expertly selected wines that complement each course. The impeccable service and the refined atmosphere ensure a memorable evening.

Ristorante Villa del Quar

Ristorante Villa del Quar, situated within the opulent Villa del Quar Relais & Châteaux, offers a dining experience that exudes sophistication and tranquility. The restaurant's menu, crafted by Chef Bruno Barbieri, showcases the best of

Italian and Veronese cuisine, with a focus on fresh, high-quality ingredients and elegant presentation. The serene setting, overlooking the lush gardens and vineyards, adds to the enchantment of the dining experience. Guests can choose from an à la carte menu or a tasting menu, with prices typically ranging from €90 to €150 per person. A key tip for visitors is to take a stroll through the villa's beautiful gardens before or after the meal, allowing time to fully appreciate the serene surroundings. The combination of exquisite cuisine, attentive service, and the picturesque setting makes Ristorante Villa del Quar a true culinary haven.

CHAPTER 7
DAY TRIPS AND EXCURSIONS

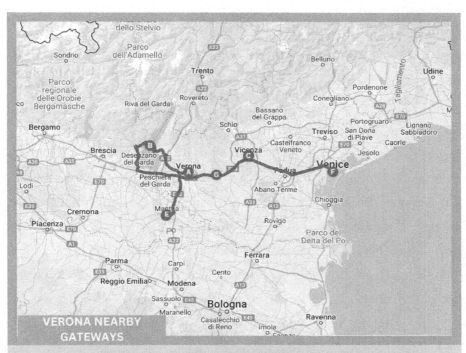

Directions from Verona, VR, Italy to Te Palace, Viale Te, Mantua, Province of Mantua, Italy

A
Verona, VR, Italy

B
Lake Garda, Italy

C
Vicenza, Province of Vicenza, Italy

D
Ville palladiane, Corso Andrea Palladio, Vicenza, Province of Vicenza, Italy

E
Mantua, Province of Mantua, Italy

F
Venice, Metropolitan City of Venice, Italy

G
Soave, VR, Italy

H
Te Palace, Viale Te, Mantua, Province of flantua, Italy

118

7.1 Lake Garda: Sirmione and Garda Town

Verona serves as a gateway to a plethora of captivating destinations, with Lake Garda standing out as a must-visit destination for travelers seeking natural beauty and historical charm. Embarking on day trips from Verona to Lake Garda offers a perfect blend of scenic vistas, cultural immersion, and culinary delights, promising an unforgettable experience for visitors.

Sirmione

One of the most enchanting excursions from Verona is a journey to Sirmione, a picturesque town situated at the southern tip of Lake Garda. Accessible by car or train, Sirmione beckons travelers with its stunning medieval castle, Scaliger Castle, which stands proudly at the entrance to the town. Visitors can explore the narrow streets lined with quaint shops and cafes, bask in the therapeutic waters of the thermal baths at Terme di Sirmione, or take a leisurely stroll along the lakeside promenade. The cost of transportation to Sirmione varies depending on the mode of travel, but it typically ranges from €10 to €20 per person for a round-trip journey.

Garda Town

Another captivating destination for day trips from Verona is Garda Town, located on the southeastern shores of Lake Garda. Offering a serene ambiance and rich history, Garda Town entices visitors with its charming harbor, lively piazzas, and ancient churches. Travelers can delve into the town's past by visiting landmarks such as the Church of San Nicolò and the Palazzo dei Capitani, or simply unwind by the waterfront while savoring gelato or traditional Italian cuisine. The distance from Verona to Garda Town is approximately 40 kilometers, and transportation costs range from €15 to €25 per person for a round-trip journey by train or bus.

Malcesine

For those seeking outdoor adventure amidst breathtaking scenery, a day trip to Malcesine from Verona is a must. Situated on the northeastern shores of Lake Garda, Malcesine captivates visitors with its medieval charm and panoramic views of the surrounding mountains. The highlight of a visit to Malcesine is a ride on the Monte Baldo Cable Car, which transports travelers to the summit of Monte Baldo for sweeping vistas of the lake and beyond. Additionally, adrenaline junkies can indulge in water sports such as windsurfing or sailing, while culture enthusiasts can explore the historic streets and landmarks like the Scaliger Castle. Transportation costs to Malcesine typically range from €20 to €30 per person for a round-trip journey by train or bus.

Bardolino

Wine lovers seeking a taste of Italy's renowned viticulture will find delight in a day trip to Bardolino from Verona. Located on the eastern shores of Lake Garda, Bardolino is synonymous with world-class wine production, particularly its namesake Bardolino wine. Visitors can embark on guided tours of local wineries, where they can sample an array of wines while learning about the region's winemaking traditions. Beyond wine tasting, Bardolino offers scenic waterfront promenades, charming cafes, and cultural attractions such as the Church of San Severo and the Olive Oil Museum. The distance from Verona to Bardolino is approximately 30 kilometers, and transportation costs range from €15 to €25 per person for a round-trip journey by train or bus.

Riva del Garda

For an exhilarating day trip filled with outdoor pursuits and natural wonders, Riva del Garda beckons from the northern shores of Lake Garda. Surrounded by towering mountains and crystal-clear waters, Riva del Garda is a haven for outdoor enthusiasts, offering opportunities for hiking, mountain biking, and rock climbing. Visitors can explore the historic town center with its charming squares and medieval buildings, or embark on a scenic boat cruise to admire the lake's stunning landscapes. Additionally, Riva del Garda hosts various events and festivals throughout the year, showcasing the region's rich cultural heritage. The distance from Verona to Riva del Garda is approximately 80 kilometers, and transportation costs range from €20 to €35 per person for a round-trip journey by train or bus.

7.2 Vicenza and Palladian Villas

Verona itself offers a plethora of attractions to delve into, venturing beyond its borders unveils a treasure trove of experiences waiting to be discovered. From the historic city of Vicenza to the breathtaking Palladian Villas scattered throughout the countryside, there are several captivating day trips and excursions that promise to enrich your Italian journey.

Vicenza

Embark on a journey to Vicenza, a city renowned for its architectural masterpieces and rich cultural heritage. Situated approximately 60 kilometers east of Verona, Vicenza is easily accessible by train, with a journey time of around 30 to 40 minutes. The cost of transportation typically ranges from €5 to €15, depending on the class of service and time of booking. Upon arrival in Vicenza, visitors are greeted by the timeless beauty of its historic center, a UNESCO World Heritage Site. Marvel at the elegant facades of buildings designed by the illustrious architect Andrea Palladio, whose influence is omnipresent throughout the city. Take a leisurely stroll along the Corso Andrea Palladio, lined with palaces, churches, and monuments that showcase the architectural genius of the Renaissance era.

A highlight of any visit to Vicenza is exploring the iconic Palladian Villas scattered across the Veneto countryside. These splendid country estates, designed by Palladio himself, epitomize the harmonious blend of art, architecture, and nature. From the grandeur of Villa Capra "La Rotonda" to the serenity of Villa Barbaro in nearby Maser, each villa offers a unique glimpse into the opulent lifestyle of Venetian nobility.

Immersive Cultural Experiences in Vicenza

In addition to its architectural wonders, Vicenza boasts a vibrant cultural scene that captivates visitors of all interests. Art enthusiasts can admire masterpieces by Venetian painters at the Civic Art Gallery, while history buffs can delve into the city's past at the Museo di Palazzo Chiericati. For a taste of local life, wander through the bustling markets of Piazza dei Signori or savor traditional Venetian cuisine at one of the city's charming trattorias.As the day draws to a close, bask in the golden glow of the setting sun illuminating Vicenza's picturesque streets before boarding the train back to Verona. Reflecting on the day's adventures, you'll carry with you memories of timeless beauty and cultural richness that define the essence of the Veneto region.

7.3 Mantua: Ducal Palace and Palazzo Te

Mantua stands out as an unforgettable experience, promising a tapestry of Renaissance architecture, rich cultural heritage, and scenic landscapes. As travelers venture beyond the cobblestone streets of Verona, they are met with the allure of Mantua's historic treasures, including the majestic Ducal Palace and the breathtaking Palazzo Te. The journey from Verona to Mantua is approximately 40 miles (64 kilometers), making it easily accessible for a day trip by various modes of transportation. Travelers can opt for a scenic train ride, with regular departures from Verona Porta Nuova station to Mantua's centrally located train station. Alternatively, those seeking flexibility can embark on a picturesque drive, enjoying the Italian countryside along the way. Rental cars are readily available in Verona, providing the freedom to explore at one's own pace.

Exploring Mantua

Upon arrival in Mantua, visitors are greeted by a city steeped in history and brimming with architectural marvels. The UNESCO-listed historic center, surrounded by tranquil lakes, sets the stage for a captivating journey through time. A stroll along the cobblestone streets reveals a treasure trove of Renaissance palaces, churches, and piazzas, each bearing witness to Mantua's illustrious past as a flourishing cultural hub.

Ducal Palace

One of Mantua's crowning jewels is the imposing Ducal Palace, a masterpiece of Renaissance architecture and a testament to the city's noble heritage. Built over centuries by the powerful Gonzaga family, the palace exudes grandeur at every turn. Visitors can marvel at its magnificent frescoed chambers, adorned with works by renowned artists such as Mantegna and Pisanello. A guided tour offers insight into the palace's storied history, from its medieval origins to its role as a symbol of Gonzaga power.

Palazzo Te

For a glimpse into the opulent lifestyle of Mantua's ruling elite, a visit to Palazzo Te is a must. Situated on the outskirts of the city, this architectural gem showcases the lavish tastes of Duke Federico II Gonzaga. Designed by the celebrated architect Giulio Romano, the palace is a masterpiece of Mannerist design, featuring intricately decorated rooms, lush gardens, and stunning frescoes. Highlights include the iconic Sala dei Giganti, where Romano's illusionistic paintings transport visitors to a realm of myth and legend.

Cost of Transportation and Admission

Travelers can expect to budget around €10-15 for a one-way train ticket from Verona to Mantua, with slight variations depending on the class of service and time of booking. Entrance fees to attractions such as the Ducal Palace and

Palazzo Te typically range from €10-15 per person, with discounts available for students, seniors, and groups. Guided tours may incur additional costs, but offer invaluable insights into Mantua's rich cultural heritage.

7.4 Venice: The Floating City

Venturing from the romantic streets of Verona to the captivating waterways of Venice offers travelers a journey into a world unlike any other. Often dubbed "The Floating City," Venice beckons with its timeless charm, rich history, and unparalleled beauty, making it an essential day trip destination for those visiting Verona.

Venice

Embarking on a day trip from Verona to Venice unveils a tapestry of delights for the senses. As the iconic gondolas glide gracefully along the labyrinthine canals, visitors are transported to a bygone era of opulence and intrigue. The journey from Verona to Venice is approximately 120 kilometers, and travelers can opt for various transportation modes, including trains or buses, with costs ranging from €10 to €30 per person for a round-trip journey. Upon arrival in Venice, travelers are greeted by the grandeur of St. Mark's Square, the city's bustling centerpiece. Here, they can marvel at architectural wonders such as St. Mark's Basilica and the Doge's Palace, symbols of Venice's storied past as a maritime powerhouse. Exploring the winding alleyways and hidden courtyards, visitors will encounter quaint cafes, artisan boutiques, and local artisans practicing age-old crafts, offering a glimpse into Venetian daily life.

Mantua

For a journey off the beaten path, travelers can venture from Verona to Mantua, a UNESCO World Heritage Site renowned for its Renaissance architecture and cultural heritage. Nestled amidst the picturesque landscape of the Lombardy region, Mantua beckons with its charming piazzas, elegant palaces, and historic landmarks. The distance from Verona to Mantua is approximately 45 kilometers, and transportation costs range from €10 to €20 per person for a round-trip journey by train or bus. Exploring Mantua's historic center, visitors can marvel at architectural marvels such as the Palazzo Ducale, home to the Gonzaga family, and the magnificent Basilica of Sant'Andrea, designed by renowned architect Leon Battista Alberti. Art enthusiasts will delight in the city's wealth of museums and galleries, including the Palazzo Te, adorned with frescoes by the legendary artist, Giulio Romano. Additionally, food lovers can savor Mantua's culinary delights, from traditional dishes like tortelli di zucca to decadent pastries like sbrisolona.

Padua

Just a short distance from Verona lies Padua, a vibrant university city brimming with history, art, and innovation. Renowned for its prestigious university, founded in 1222, Padua boasts a rich intellectual heritage that is reflected in its magnificent landmarks and cultural institutions. The journey from Verona to Padua is approximately 80 kilometers, and transportation costs range from €15 to €25 per person for a round-trip journey by train or bus. Upon arrival in Padua, visitors can explore the city's historic center, where treasures such as the Scrovegni Chapel, adorned with frescoes by Giotto, and the imposing Palazzo della Ragione await. Nature lovers can wander through the enchanting Botanical Garden, the oldest in the world, while shoppers can peruse the bustling markets and boutiques that line the streets. Additionally, Padua offers a vibrant culinary scene, with traditional trattorias and contemporary eateries serving up a feast of flavors

Bassano del Grappa

For a taste of rural charm and natural beauty, travelers can journey from Verona to Bassano del Grappa, a picturesque town nestled in the foothills of the Venetian Prealps. Famous for its namesake spirit, grappa, Bassano del Grappa boasts a scenic setting, with the Brenta River winding through its historic center. The distance from Verona to Bassano del Grappa is approximately 90 kilometers, and transportation costs range from €20 to €30 per person for a round-trip journey by train or bus. Exploring Bassano del Grappa, visitors can stroll across the town's iconic Ponte degli Alpini, a covered wooden bridge dating back to the 16th century, offering panoramic views of the surrounding countryside. Art aficionados will appreciate the town's museums and galleries, which showcase works by local and renowned artists alike. Additionally, food and wine enthusiasts can sample regional specialties such as Asiago cheese and Polenta alla Bassanese, paired with a glass of locally-produced grappa.

7.5 Soave and Wine Country

Just a stone's throw away from the bustling streets of Verona, this picturesque landscape is dotted with vineyards, medieval villages, and centuries-old wineries, offering an idyllic escape for wine enthusiasts and explorers alike.

Soave

Embark on a journey to Soave, a charming medieval town renowned for its eponymous white wine and enchanting hilltop castle. Situated approximately 25 kilometers east of Verona, Soave is easily accessible by car or train, with a journey time of around 30 to 40 minutes. The cost of transportation varies depending on the mode of travel, with train tickets typically costing between €5 to €10. Upon arrival in Soave, visitors are greeted by the timeless allure of its historic center, characterized by narrow cobblestone streets and ancient stone walls. Wander through the winding alleyways, adorned with colorful flowers cascading from wrought-iron balconies, and soak in the atmosphere of old-world charm. Ascend to the summit of the medieval castle, where panoramic views of the surrounding vineyards and rolling hills await, providing the perfect backdrop for a memorable photo opportunity.

Wine Tasting in the Heart of Verona's Vineyards

No visit to Verona's wine country would be complete without indulging in a wine tasting experience amidst the region's lush vineyards. From family-run estates to renowned wineries, there are countless opportunities to sample the rich diversity of wines produced in the area, including the famed Soave Classico DOC. Visitors can embark on guided tours of the vineyards, learn about the winemaking process firsthand, and savor the flavors of locally-produced wines, accompanied by delectable regional cuisine.

Exploring the Countryside: Beyond Soave

Venture beyond the confines of Soave to explore the picturesque countryside that surrounds Verona, where vine-covered hillsides and quaint villages beckon travelers to embark on a journey of discovery. Drive along scenic country roads lined with rows of vines, stopping along the way to explore charming towns such as Monteforte d'Alpone and San Pietro in Cariano. Immerse yourself in the tranquility of rural life, where time seems to stand still amidst the timeless beauty of the landscape.

Outdoor Activities and Cultural Experiences

In addition to wine tasting and sightseeing, Verona's wine country offers a plethora of outdoor activities and cultural experiences to suit every taste. From hiking and cycling through the vineyards to attending local festivals and events celebrating the region's rich heritage, there's no shortage of ways to immerse yourself in the local culture. Visit historic landmarks such as the Villa Serego Alighieri, once home to the descendants of Dante Alighieri, or explore the ancient Roman ruins at nearby Gavi.

CHAPTER 8
ENTERTAINMENT AND NIGHTLIFE

8.1 Piazza Bra: Bars and Terraces

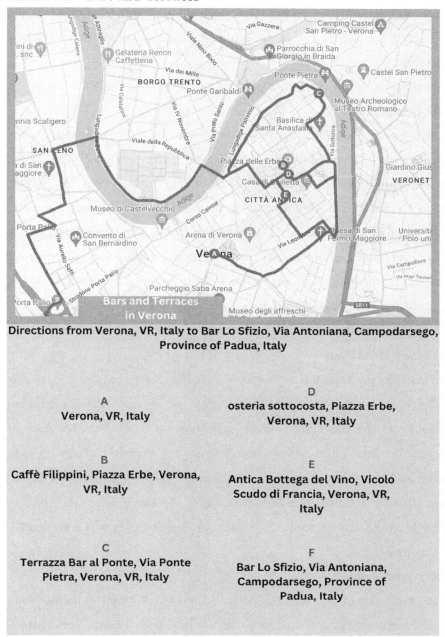

Directions from Verona, VR, Italy to Bar Lo Sfizio, Via Antoniana, Campodarsego, Province of Padua, Italy

A
Verona, VR, Italy

B
Caffè Filippini, Piazza Erbe, Verona, VR, Italy

C
Terrazza Bar al Ponte, Via Ponte Pietra, Verona, VR, Italy

D
osteria sottocosta, Piazza Erbe, Verona, VR, Italy

E
Antica Bottega del Vino, Vicolo Scudo di Francia, Verona, VR, Italy

F
Bar Lo Sfizio, Via Antoniana, Campodarsego, Province of Padua, Italy

As dusk descends upon the picturesque city of Verona, Italy, Piazza Bra awakens with a lively energy that beckons both locals and visitors alike to immerse themselves in its vibrant nightlife and entertainment scene. Piazza Bra boasts an array of charming bars and terraces, each offering a unique atmosphere and experience that captures the essence of Italian hospitality and culture.

Caffè Filippini

Located on the eastern edge of Piazza Bra, Caffè Filippini exudes a classic Italian charm that draws patrons in with its inviting ambiance and delectable aperitivo offerings. As the sun sets over Verona, locals gather on the outdoor terrace to indulge in traditional spritz cocktails paired with an array of mouthwatering cicchetti. The laid-back atmosphere and warm hospitality make Caffè Filippini the perfect spot to unwind after a day of exploring the city. Prices here are reasonable, allowing visitors to enjoy the true essence of Italian hospitality without breaking the bank.

Terrazza Bar Al Ponte

For those seeking breathtaking views of Verona's iconic landmarks, Terrazza Bar Al Ponte is a must-visit destination. Perched on the edge of Piazza Bra overlooking the historic Roman amphitheater, this rooftop bar offers unparalleled panoramas of the cityscape below. Guests can sip on expertly crafted cocktails while taking in the enchanting sight of the illuminated Arena di Verona against the backdrop of the starlit sky. Although prices may be slightly higher here, the unforgettable experience and mesmerizing views are well worth the investment.

Osteria Sottocosta

As the night progresses, the cobblestone streets of Piazza Bra come alive with the infectious rhythms of live music emanating from Osteria Sottocosta. This lively venue offers an eclectic mix of entertainment, from jazz and blues performances to DJ sets that keep the dance floor packed until the early hours of the morning. The intimate setting and warm ambiance create the perfect environment for mingling with locals and fellow travelers alike, making Osteria Sottocosta a hotspot for experiencing Verona's dynamic nightlife scene. While prices for drinks and snacks may vary depending on the evening's entertainment, the vibrant atmosphere and energetic vibe make it a worthwhile destination for music lovers and night owls alike.

Antica Bottega Del Vino

For a taste of Verona's rich cultural heritage, look no further than Antica Bottega Del Vino. This historic wine bar, located just steps away from Piazza Bra, has been serving up fine wines and gourmet cuisine since 1890. Step inside and be transported back in time as you admire the elegant decor and charming ambiance reminiscent of a bygone era. Sample an exquisite selection of local wines paired with artisanal cheeses and cured meats while soaking in the intimate atmosphere of this beloved Veronese institution. Prices here may be higher compared to other establishments, but the opportunity to indulge in a true taste of Italian culture and tradition makes it a worthwhile investment for discerning travelers.

Bar Lo Sfizio

As the clock strikes midnight, the party shows no signs of slowing down at Bar Lo Sfizio. Tucked away in a corner of Piazza Bra, this lively bar is a favorite among locals for its energetic atmosphere and late-night revelry. Whether you're in the mood for a classic cocktail or a refreshing pint of beer, you'll find no shortage of libations to keep the festivities going well into the early hours of the morning. Prices here are affordable, allowing patrons to indulge in a night of celebration without breaking the bank. With its eclectic mix of music, friendly clientele, and lively ambiance, Bar Lo Sfizio offers an authentic taste of Verona's nightlife that is not to be missed.

8.2 Opera at the Arena di Verona

As you step into the grandeur of the Arena di Verona, the city is alive with anticipation, echoing the vibrant history and cultural richness of Verona. This is not just any night; this is a night at the opera, an experience that transcends time and transports you to a world of passion, drama, and pure magic.

The Arena di Verona

Arena di Verona stands as a testament to the enduring legacy of ancient Roman architecture. Built in the 1st century AD, this magnificent amphitheater has witnessed centuries of history, from gladiatorial contests to medieval jousts, and now, it serves as the enchanting backdrop for world-class opera performances.

Opera Under the Stars

As twilight falls and the stars emerge, the Arena di Verona comes to life with the melodious strains of opera. Imagine taking your seat beneath the open sky, surrounded by the ancient stone walls that have stood the test of time. The stage is set, the lights dim, and then, the music begins. From Verdi to Puccini, the voices of world-renowned singers fill the air, weaving tales of love, betrayal, and redemption that resonate deep within your soul.

Embracing Tradition

Attending an opera at the Arena di Verona is not just a night out; it's an immersive cultural experience that immerses you in the rich tapestry of Italian heritage. From the moment you enter the arena, you become part of a tradition that stretches back centuries, a tradition of artistic excellence and passionate storytelling. And the best part? Despite its grandeur, opera at the Arena di Verona remains surprisingly accessible, with ticket prices catering to a wide range of budgets.

Unique Features

What sets opera at the Arena di Verona apart from any other theatrical experience is its unparalleled atmosphere. There's something truly magical about witnessing a performance under the twinkling stars, surrounded by history and beauty at every turn. From the acoustics that amplify every note to the breathtaking scenery that unfolds before your eyes, every moment spent at the Arena di Verona is etched into your memory forever.

8.3 Live Music Venues and Jazz Clubs

As the sun dips below Verona's ancient skyline, the city undergoes a magical transformation, unveiling its vibrant nocturnal soul. For those seeking to immerse themselves in the rhythmic heartbeat of this enchanting Italian city after dusk, exploring its live music venues and jazz clubs becomes an exhilarating odyssey through sound and sensation.

Discovering Verona's Musical Enclaves

Verona are an array of live music venues and jazz clubs, each offering a unique sonic experience that resonates with the city's rich cultural tapestry. Venturing into these hidden gems unveils a world where melody and rhythm converge to create unforgettable moments of euphoria.

The Harmonious Haven of Casa di Giulietta

Steeped in romantic lore, Casa di Giulietta serves as more than a mere backdrop to Shakespeare's timeless tale of love; it's also home to Verona's burgeoning music scene. As the moon rises overhead, this historic courtyard transforms into an intimate stage where local musicians captivate audiences with soul-stirring performances. Here, amidst the whispers of star-crossed lovers, visitors can savor the melodies of Verona's burgeoning talent while basking in the ethereal ambiance of Juliet's balcony.

Embracing the Jazz Jive at Cantina del Duomo

Tucked away in the heart of Verona's historic center lies Cantina del Duomo, a cozy cellar-turned-jazz club that exudes old-world charm and sophistication. Descending into this subterranean sanctuary, guests are greeted by the sultry notes of live jazz, weaving a seductive tapestry of rhythm and blues. With its dimly lit ambiance and eclectic selection of wines, Cantina del Duomo offers an immersive experience that transports visitors to a bygone era of jazz-age glamour.

Swaying to the Beat at Jazz Club Verona

For aficionados of the genre, Jazz Club Verona stands as a beacon of musical excellence, drawing in crowds with its electrifying performances and dynamic atmosphere. Located in the heart of Verona's historic district, this iconic venue boasts an impressive lineup of local and international jazz artists, ensuring an unforgettable evening of sonic exploration. From smooth saxophone solos to lively improvisations, Jazz Club Verona promises a sensory journey through the diverse landscape of jazz.

Dancing the Night Away at Osteria del Bugiardo

As the night unfolds, Osteria del Bugiardo emerges as a hotspot for revelers seeking to dance beneath the stars. With its eclectic blend of live music and vibrant atmosphere, this lively osteria offers a taste of Verona's contemporary music scene. From energetic rock bands to soulful acoustic sets, Osteria del Bugiardo sets the stage for unforgettable nights filled with laughter, camaraderie, and boundless joy.

Immersing in Verona's Musical Tapestry

In the heart of Verona's historic streets lies a world of musical discovery waiting to be explored. From intimate courtyard concerts to lively jazz clubs, the city's nightlife scene offers something for every musical palate. Whether you're a jazz aficionado or simply seeking to soak in the vibrant ambiance of Verona after dark, embarking on a nocturnal journey through its live music venues promises to be an experience like no other. So, as the stars begin to twinkle overhead, let the melodies of Verona serenade you into the night, and immerse yourself in the timeless allure of this enchanting Italian city.

8.4 Nightlife in Veronetta and Piazza delle Erbe

Verona's nightlife scene offers a diverse array of experiences, from charming taverns and wine bars in Veronetta to elegant cafés and cocktail lounges in Piazza delle Erbe. Whether you're sipping on fine wines, dancing the night away, or simply soaking in the ambiance of this enchanting city, Verona promises an unforgettable night of excitement and adventure that will leave you longing to return time and time again.

Veronetta's Taverns and Wine Bars

On the opposite side of the Adige River, away from the bustling crowds of the city center, lies the charming neighborhood of Veronetta. Here, amidst narrow cobblestone streets and historic buildings, you'll discover a treasure trove of taverns and wine bars waiting to be explored. One such gem is Osteria del Bugiardo, a cozy tavern known for its extensive wine list and rustic Italian cuisine. Step inside and be greeted by the warm glow of candlelight and the inviting aroma of freshly prepared dishes. Prices here are reasonable, allowing patrons to indulge in a night of culinary delights without breaking the bank. Whether you're sampling local wines or savoring traditional Venetian cicchetti, Osteria del Bugiardo offers an authentic taste of Veronetta's vibrant culinary scene.

Piazza delle Erbe's Cafés and Cocktail Bars

In the heart of Verona's historic city center lies Piazza delle Erbe, a bustling square brimming with life and energy. Here, amidst the stunning architecture and vibrant street vendors, you'll find an array of charming cafés and cocktail bars that beckon you to linger and soak in the atmosphere. One such establishment is Bar al Portico, a quaint café nestled beneath the arches of a centuries-old portico. Pull up a chair on the outdoor terrace and watch as the world passes by while sipping on a freshly brewed espresso or a refreshing Aperol Spritz. Prices here are affordable, making it the perfect spot to unwind after a day of sightseeing or shopping in the nearby market stalls. With its relaxed ambiance and prime location, Bar al Portico captures the timeless elegance of Piazza delle Erbe and invites visitors to experience the magic of Verona's historic city center.

Casa Perbellini's Mixology Bar

For a taste of luxury and sophistication, look no further than Casa Perbellini's Mixology Bar. Located just steps away from Piazza delle Erbe, this stylish cocktail lounge offers an elevated drinking experience unlike any other in Verona. Step inside and be transported to a world of refined elegance, where expert mixologists craft innovative cocktails using only the finest ingredients. Prices here may be higher compared to other establishments, but the impeccable service and exquisite drinks make it a worthwhile investment for discerning travelers. Whether you're sipping on a classic Negroni or sampling one of their signature creations, Casa Perbellini's Mixology Bar promises an unforgettable night of indulgence and sophistication.

Dance the Night Away at Club Nero

As the sun sets and the stars emerge overhead, the streets of Verona come alive with the pulsating beats of Club Nero. Located in the heart of Veronetta, this vibrant nightclub is a favorite among locals and visitors alike for its energetic atmosphere and top-notch DJ lineup. Step inside and let the music wash over you as you dance the night away on the crowded dance floor. Prices for drinks and entry may vary depending on the evening's events, but the electrifying energy and lively ambiance make it a worthwhile destination for partygoers seeking an unforgettable night out in Verona.

La Bottega del Buon Caffè

For a taste of Verona's bohemian side, venture into the eclectic neighborhood of Veronetta and discover the laid-back charm of La Bottega del Buon Caffè. This cozy café and cocktail bar exudes a relaxed vibe that invites patrons to linger and unwind in its cozy interiors. Whether you're sipping on a freshly brewed coffee or indulging in a craft cocktail, La Bottega del Buon Caffè offers a welcoming atmosphere and friendly service that captures the essence of Verona's vibrant cultural scene. Prices here are reasonable, making it the perfect spot to escape the hustle and bustle of the city and immerse yourself in the laid-back charm of Veronetta.

8.5 Cultural Events: Festivals and Concerts

Verona offers a plethora of venues for experiencing the magic of live performances, festivals, and concerts throughout the year.

Verona Opera Festival: Step into the enchanting world of opera at the Verona Opera Festival, held annually in August at the iconic Arena di Verona. This world-renowned event draws opera lovers from around the globe to witness spectacular performances against the backdrop of the ancient Roman amphitheater. From classic operas by Verdi and Puccini to modern interpretations, the Verona Opera Festival promises an unforgettable journey through the depths of human emotion, all under the starlit sky.

Verona Jazz Festival: In June, Verona becomes a haven for jazz enthusiasts as it hosts the Verona Jazz Festival, a celebration of improvisation, rhythm, and soulful melodies. Set against the picturesque backdrop of historic landmarks and scenic vistas, this festival brings together international jazz artists and local talents for electrifying performances that ignite the senses. From intimate club settings to outdoor concerts in charming squares, the Verona Jazz Festival offers a diverse range of experiences for music lovers of all ages.

Tocati: For a taste of whimsy and nostalgia, look no further than Tocati, Verona's annual festival dedicated to traditional games and play. Held in September, Tocati transforms the streets of Verona into a playground of laughter and joy, where visitors can engage in ancient pastimes, from street chess to medieval archery. With interactive workshops, live performances, and exhibitions showcasing games from around the world, Tocati is a delightful celebration of fun and camaraderie that captivates audiences of all ages.

Verona Arena Summer Festival: Experience the magic of classical music at the Verona Arena Summer Festival, a series of concerts held from June to September at the historic Arena di Verona. Against the backdrop of ancient Roman architecture, world-class orchestras and soloists take center stage, performing masterpieces by Mozart, Beethoven, and more. Whether you're a seasoned classical music aficionado or a casual listener, the Verona Arena Summer Festival offers an enchanting opportunity to revel in the timeless beauty of symphonic music beneath the starry Veronese sky.

Verona Film Festival: Lights, camera, action! Every October, Verona plays host to its annual Film Festival, a cinematic celebration that showcases the best of Italian and international cinema. From thought-provoking documentaries to captivating dramas, the Verona Film Festival offers a diverse lineup of screenings, discussions, and special events that inspire, entertain, and provoke conversation. Whether you're a film buff or simply curious to explore the world of cinema, the Verona Film Festival invites you to immerse yourself in the magic of storytelling on the silver screen.

CONCLUSION AND RECOMMENDATIONS

As the final pages of *"Verona Pocket Travel Guide 2024"* draw to a close, I find myself reflecting on the myriad experiences that have shaped my journey through this enchanting city. Verona, with its timeless charm and rich cultural heritage, has a way of captivating the soul and leaving an indelible mark on all who wander its storied streets. As I bid farewell to this jewel of Northern Italy, I am compelled to share some insider tips and heartfelt insights for fellow travelers embarking on their own adventure to Verona.

Recommendations:

Embrace the Magic of Off-Peak Hours: While Verona's main attractions are undoubtedly breathtaking, consider exploring them during off-peak hours to avoid the crowds and truly savor the experience. Early mornings and late evenings offer a serene ambiance that allows for a deeper connection with the city's historic landmarks.

Indulge in Culinary Delights Beyond the Piazza: While Verona's piazzas offer a plethora of dining options, don't hesitate to venture off the beaten path and discover hidden trattorias and osterias tucked away in quiet alleyways. Here, you'll find authentic Italian cuisine served with a side of genuine hospitality, providing a taste of Verona's culinary soul.

Immerse Yourself in Local Culture: Beyond the iconic sights, take the time to immerse yourself in Verona's vibrant cultural scene. Attend a performance at the Arena di Verona or explore the city's museums and galleries to gain a deeper understanding of its rich artistic heritage. Engaging with locals and participating in cultural events will enrich your experience and leave you with lasting memories.

Stroll Through Verona's Neighborhoods: Venture beyond the historic center and explore Verona's diverse neighborhoods, each with its own unique character and charm. From the medieval streets of San Zeno to the bohemian vibe of Veronetta, meandering through these lesser-known areas offers a glimpse into everyday life in Verona and provides opportunities for unexpected encounters and discoveries.

Embrace Serendipity: While it's essential to have a rough itinerary, leave room for spontaneity and serendipitous encounters along the way. Some of the most memorable moments in Verona are often found off the beaten path, whether it's stumbling upon a hidden garden or striking up a conversation with a friendly local.

So, dear traveler, heed the call of Verona's siren song, and let its timeless beauty beckon you to embark on an adventure of a lifetime. For in the embrace of Verona's embrace, you'll find not only a city but a home for the heart!

Printed in Great Britain
by Amazon